O Soul at peace,
return to your Lord,
well-pleased,
well-pleasing!
Join My servants!
Enter My Paradise!

– Qur'an: 89:29-30

Presented to ....

....

From ....

Date ....

Also by Ruqaiyyah Waris Maqsood

After Death, Life!

Thoughts to alleviate the grief of all Muslims facing death and bereavement

Ruqaiyyah Waris Maqsood

Goodword
B·O·O·K·S

Dedicated to
my dear friend and sister,
Zarina Choudry,
with thanks for all her help and
encouragement and love to me,
and to so many others.

First published in 1998
© Goodword Books 2002
Reprinted 1999, 2000, 2002

Goodword Books Pvt. Ltd.
1, Nizamuddin West Market
New Delhi 110 013
Tel. 435 5454, 435 6666
Fax 435 7333, 435 7980
e-mail: info@goodwordbooks.com
www.goodwordbooks.com

Contents

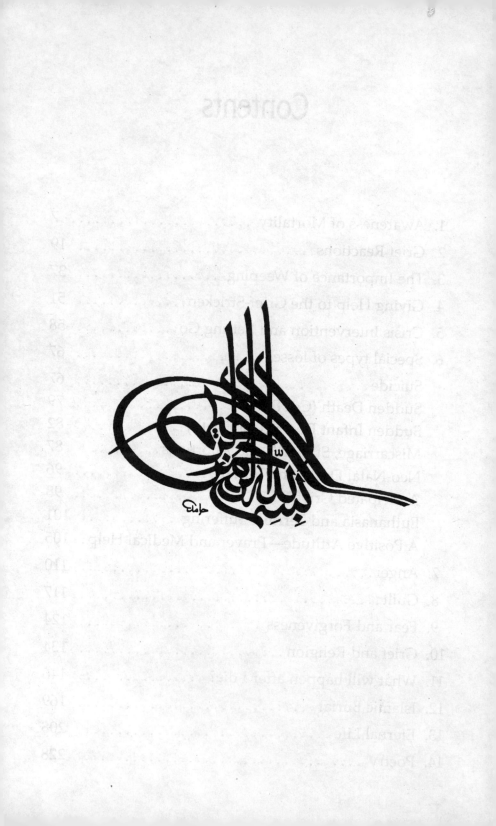

Chapter 1

Awareness of Mortality

Every day, hundreds of people are suddenly forced to come to terms with their mortality; perhaps someone they love has passed away as the result of illness or old age; there may have been a tragic accident, somebody killed by machinery, or fire or flood. The media tug our heartstrings with terrible pictures of war victims, or those abandoned to famine. Maybe an individual has not felt very well for some time and has been unable to 'pull out of it'. It is only natural to visit the doctor hoping to be given some cure, some medicine that will solve the problem—but perhaps this time the news is that which is most feared, which strikes the heart with terror and shock. There comes a day in the life of all people when they are obliged to live with the knowledge that they are going to die.

Death, and bereavement through death, has to be faced as a fact of life. We cannot prevent it. It makes no difference whether we are good or evil, noble or despicable, a devout believer or an atheist. It makes no difference if we have avoided the thought before; we always hope that death will not happen to us yet, will not disrupt our family, our marriage—but of course we know in our hearts that ultimately there is no avoiding it, and we are not consulted to see if we are ready for it. It usually catches us out, even if we know that from the moment we are conceived our life is a journey, one that will come to an end. In fact, we could say that from the moment of our birth, we are dying. The fact that we will die is the *only* fact we can know for sure about our own futures. It is a sobering thought.

As young people we all spend time wondering what we will do when we 'grow up', what we will achieve, what successes we will have. We all have a tendency to assume that we *will* grow up. We forget that no-one has the right to assume that they will live three-score years and ten, and die in the fulness of old age. Indeed, we have not the slightest idea of what it is that will kill us—whether we will succumb to some unpleasant disease, or die in perfect health—catching a bullet in war, perishing in fire or flood, being caught out by some accident.

The notion that any human being can know what lies ahead of them is completely false, an illusion. I often used to ask my young students how many of them knew what they were going to have for their evening meal, or how they were going to get home after the class. Most of them would put up their hands with a confident answer. Only a few would hesitate, knowing that I have a fondness for 'trick questions'. The next question, of course, was how many of them actually knew that they *would* be having their evening meal, or would be arriving at their homes for sure? This time, the raised hands were quavering a little—

they were not so confident.

For the truth, as opposed to the illusion, is that no person knows their future, what will happen in the next minute, never mind the next evening or next day. As Muslims, we should always remember when we predict of anything that it will come to pass, to add 'Insha' Allah'—'if Allah wills' (18:23-24). This is one of the basic concepts of Islam—that only Allah, the Eternal, the Ever-Living, the Absolute, has this knowledge.

> 'Truly, nothing is hidden from Allah on earth
> or in the heavens. It is He who shapes you in
> the wombs as He pleases.' (3:5-6).

It is Allah alone Who knows the answer to every single thing; and our share of that knowledge is no more nor less than He chooses to reveal to us.

This is made very clear in the ringing words of ayat al-Kursi, the Throne:

> 'Allah, the Everliving, the Self-Subsisting, the
> Eternal; there is no God but He! He neither
> slumbers nor sleeps. Everything in the heav-
> ens and earth belongs to Him. Who can inter-
> cede in His presence except as He wills? He
> knows what lies before us and what is hidden
> from us, and we cannot gain knowledge of
> anything except as He wills. For His is the
> kingdom, the power and the glory, and He
> guards and preserves the heavens and the
> earth without weariness; for He is the Most
> High, the Most Glorious One.' (2:255).

This is a very important point to take in when we are confronted with the trauma of what seems to be a 'medical death-sentence'. Only a person who has actually gone through the horror of discovering they have an incurable disease can fully understand the dreadful terror of that moment; the cold claws grasping the pit of the stomach, the nausea and shock. Those who have not had this experience can murmur their sympathy, but they cannot really feel it.

But the Muslim should find comfort in two things: firstly, the realisation that our knowledge and that of every human is limited, and secondly that the knowledge of Allah is not. He knows the time of our death and our fates, even while we are still in the womb. 'Allah knows what every female (womb) is bearing, by how much the wombs fall short or do exceed. Every single thing is before His sight, in proportion.' (13:8)

One tradition even suggests that Allah knows it even before our conception. Aishah recorded that on one occasion, when the Prophet was called to lead the funeral prayer for the baby of one of his Ansari friends, she commented that it would surely find happiness as one of the 'birds of paradise,' since it had never committed a sin. The Prophet replied gravely that even so it might be otherwise, for God created those who are fit for Heaven or Hell while they were still in their father's loins—even before the act of intercourse in which they were conceived. (Muslim 6436 & Abu Dawud 4696).

Our lack of knowledge of our future can lead us to some foolish misconceptions, reactions to life's traumas that are quite misplaced. Let me give an example of what I mean.

Imagine two people, two women, sitting together in a hospital canteen—they came in with exactly the same symptoms, discomfort—dyspepsia, and cessation of their menses. After their consultations, the outcomes are very different—one has just been told that she has an incurable cancer, and the other that her pregnancy test has proved positive and she will bear a child. The face of the one is grey and drawn, the soul heavy and the expression bleak; the more fortunate woman is radiant and glowing, full of excitement and high hopes. They finish their tea, and step out together into the bright sunlight of the street outside. Life seems to be holding out to them such different fortunes, and we rejoice with the bearer of new life and shrink away sadly from the woman smitten with disease.

In fact, our pity and our envy are quite misplaced, and based on our human ignorance. Things may not turn out as imagined. The woman with cancer may live a further thirty years, whereas the healthy, pregnant young woman may die in an accident within the week.

Like Khadijah and the Blessed Prophet Muhammad ﷺ, I married a man considerably younger than myself. I used to be tormented by worries as to what would happen to him when I died, always foolishly assuming that because of our age difference I would leave this earth long before him. My husband used to get quite angry with me—and point out as an example that since he was the driver of our car and frequently went on long journeys when he was tired, he was far more likely to die before me. Neither of us could possibly know.

Seems strange, doesn't it? But life's like that! I had forgotten the concept of 'Insha 'Allah'—I would only die before my husband if that was God's will. In reality, neither I nor my husband have the least idea of what will come to pass—the only certainty we have is that Allah knows already; He knows, from the moment of our conception, the moment of the ceasing of our time-span here on this earth, so we might just as well put an end to our futile worrying about it.

Allah Alone knows and keeps a record of every-thing.

> 'His are the keys of the unseen, the treasures
> that no-one knows but He. He knows every-
> thing that there is on earth and in the waters.
> Not a leaf can fall but with His knowledge;
> there is not a speck in the darkness or depths
> of the earth, nor anything green or withered,
> but it is written in the Record.' (6:59).

On this road of human life there are so many fears—fear of losing control, fear of pain, fear of indignity, and the ultimate terror, fear of giving up the self at the moment of death. Will it be painful? Will we be alone? What will happen to us after death? There are so many questions about this—usually we worry about the enjoyments or sufferings to come because we cling to the notion that we will continue to exist with some kind of human, sensation-feeling, body-that-is-still-us. Will we find eternal bliss, or will we be snuffed out; or perhaps, will we face terrible eternal

torments for our sins and weaknesses? Will we find
those we have loved who have died before us, waiting
for us to welcome us into their celestial company? Will
those we leave behind find us again one day? Or will
we change completely, so that we will hardly know
ourselves, let alone other people? Will we still be
married to the same person, or will we be separated
from a dearly-loved spouse? What happens if we have
been married more than once? Or more than four times
(the Muslim limit of living wives)? Will we only have
one spouse in Paradise, and if so will it be our first
partner, or the best loved one? Aren't people going to
get hurt, and how would this fit in with a Paradise that
was eternal bliss? Suppose we did not like our partner
and wished to be free of him or her? Would we be
joined in a relationship not until death do us part, but
for ever and ever? Suppose we have never married?
Will we get beautiful huri as a sexual partner? Or will
we remain single? If male Muslims are given a huri,
what do female Muslims get?[1]

Contemplating death is not a pleasant prospect,
yet when death has been faced and accepted it has a
very dramatic effect on our outlook to life. The Prophet
☙ was well aware of this, and it was not for morbid
reasons that he counselled his companions to 'Remember death often!'. He knew that contemplating the
brevity of human life, the possible suddenness of its
cutting off, and the absolute importance of what would

---

1. We will consider the answers to these questions, and others, later.

follow, would help to improve a person's motivation and the quality of their existing present life.

A person who has been 'touched' by death can never be the same again. Whether it is facing up to the loss of some dearly-loved relative or friend, or being so ill oneself that one is merging more with the 'afterlife' than the life of this world, once awareness of approaching death has entered the human consciousness that person changes, and the attitude to his or her loved ones also changes. The possibility of losing life makes everything we have and love so much more precious.

We are haunted by the thought that the end of our earthly lives may leave unfinished tasks, incomplete relationships; remember the unfortunate case of Mr. Casaubon. This worthy gentleman devoted all his life to ignoring everyone around him and even laying aside his own personal needs and enjoyments, in order to compile a massive and comprehensive work of scholarship. He died—and the crates of unfinished notes were dumped by those few who mourned for him—unable to furnish his task whether they willed or not.

What about those of us who have been obliged to care for others throughout our lives? We are anxious about those we will leave behind who have depended upon us. How will they survive without us? What will they do? How will they cope?

A death is a prolonged emotional crisis for those left behind who have to pick up the threads after losing a dear one. Even if the death was calmly accepted, at the very least the circumstances of life of the bereaved change radically. At best, they are plunged into grief; at worst, if their Islam is shaky, they feel the meaning of life is lost and its structure shattered.

We know, of course, that we must all die ('Every soul will have a taste of death'—3:185), that we cannot escape it—but we have the very strong human failing that we like to think we are in control of our own lives and fates. When death strikes, an individual can no longer maintain the illusion of being inviolable, and we also have have to accept the unpleasant reality that medical experts are not omnipotent rescuers who come to put everything right at the eleventh hour and save us from our fate like the 'saviour-heroes' of films and TV. Real life and death situations, unfortunately for us, do not always have happy endings. The more realistic media programmes do bear this in mind, but unhappy endings and unsolved problems are not popular. They upset us.

To face this helplessness is very frightening. As Muslims, we are urged to accept the will of Allah with good grace and patience, but many people, when they find out that they are soon to die, are quite appalled and indignant. They protest, in agonies of outrage, 'Why me? Why should this happen to me?' In the crisis of facing up to death, people often become under- standably selfish and self-centred—as if the possibility of death should happen to everyone else, to other people's loved ones and friends, in other people's villages and streets—but not to *them*!

They have a gut reaction that something very unfair is happening to them—they have done 'nothing wrong', but 'God has picked them out' for punishment. Alternatively they may take the point of view that God has spotted something they have done and therefore marked them off for death. It takes a while for it to sink in that *everybody* has to face death at some time or other, that death is the most natural thing in the world, and comes to all.

They may feel that the sufferings involved leading up to death are a punishment from Allah for some wrongdoing—and completely forget or ignore how much our dear Prophet ﷺ suffered in his own final illness. Aishah, who held his head in her lap as he endured his fearful agony, declared: 'I do not begrudge anyone a peaceful death after having seen what Allah's Messenger ﷺ has endured! (Bukhari). He was not being punished at all—just going through what many of the rest of humanity have to go through.

In other words, suffering, anguish and pain at the time of death do not indicate any judgement on the person concerned. The other side of the coin, of course, is that it is quite wrong to assume that a person who dies a very calm and peaceful death is in a position of favour.

Dying people, and those they leave behind, have to face their own mortality, and possibly have to make sense of the apparent meaningless of a wasted life. The bereaved have to make this strongest possible demand on individual adjustment at the very time when they feel most exhausted and overwhelmed. Without faith, it is a cruel task indeed.

In fact, there is only one way in which a Muslim wishes to contemplate death, and that is in the aspect of faith and love. The whole basis for true Muslim life is ACCEPTANCE—submission to the will of God in every aspect of the person's life; in the home, at work, in the bosom of the family, at war, at business—in everything. When a person is so committed in love to our dear Lord, the various aspects of our mortality can be accepted for what they are, and not be given undue influence over us.

It does not matter to a submitted Muslim if we do not know what our future is going to be—God knows it, and our lives and souls are in His hands. It does not matter if we cannot work out how to achieve our ambitions, so long as we really do our best. God knows and understands everything, and judges us by our intentions if our actual achievements fall short. It does not matter if we do not know how long our lives will be—whether we will die old or young; it does not matter what our circumstances are, or in what place or country we are called to live out our spans—God is everywhere, and sees everything.

> 'Truly, no-one but God knows when the hour will come; He knows everything, from the source of the rain to the contents of the womb. No-one can know how much they will earn tomorrow, or in what land they are to die. In

truth, only God has full knowledge; He knows everything.' (31:34).

If we have faith, the knowledge of the inevitability of death and bereavement should not be seen as a horrible threat looming over us, but as an extremely important part of our lives, for which we can prepare ourselves to a considerable extent. Thinking and talking about death need not be morbid.

The fuller and richer the person's experience of life, the less death matters. The Muslim who is not afraid of death, is not afraid of life. Such a person has confidence that God is in control.

Chapter 2

Grief Reactions

If we lose someone close to us, such as a spouse or child, it is only natural to feel helpless and lost, like we did as infants. When a beloved husband or wife dies, or a child loses a parent, it is a key human figure on whom the mourner had based the emotional content of their life and security who has gone. No matter how strong the faith of the mourner, the ones remaining behind are left unhappy and frightened, feeling they have lost part of themselves. Without strong faith, the despair and sense of chaos may be profound.

Let us imagined a 'letter' a mourner might write to her mother, who has died suddenly. Imagine that this person had been very close to her mother, and now could not face the prospect of continuing life without her. She might say:

'Mum, I'm sitting here crying, the pain is so intense. I am so afraid of cracking up. You have been the main thing in my life all these years, how can I let you go? What is there left for me now? I am going to break into a thousand bits and vanish into the black sea of pain and loneliness.'

You can also imagine that similar thoughts might go from husband to dead wife, or vice versa.

This is the desperate cry of someone whose patient faith in God has taken such a knock that she has
lost her state of inner serenity. Look again at the
words—they are certainly heartfelt, and full of agony,
but two things are obvious. Firstly, the person is
concentrating on 'I' (the one left behind), not on the
new experiences of her mother, the departed one
(who has moved on), and secondly, there is no awareness of God's will or plan here. She says—'You (her
mother) have been the main thing in my life'. Let us
see how Islam could change the emphasis here. If
loving her mother *because of* her love for God had been
her first concern, then the mother's death would be
seen in perspective, and it would not be so painful for
this person to let her go.

The mourner grieves: 'I am crying, I am in pain, I
am cracking up, I can't let you go, nothing is left for me,
I am going to lose myself and vanish!' In fact, all
thoughts are concentrated on self, and anger and
bewilderment with the dead one for leaving. The grief
is all for the mourner's own predicament. This may be
perfectly normal and natural, but it is quite untouched
by Islam. In Islam, the natural sorrow for the passing
away of loved ones is transmuted by the faith that they
have not ceased to be, but have gone—insha' Allah—
to receive the reward for the toils and efforts of their
completed earthly tests.

The Qur'an gives an example of what I mean.
Surah 3 mentions the natural grief expressed by people
for those who have been slain as martyrs for Islam. We

have seen numerous examples in recent years—people
killed for no reason other than that they were Muslim
in many countries from Bosnia to Pakistan. Allah
comforts their families by giving the assurance that
they are not dead at all. True they have gone from
earth, but they are happy and rejoicing in the wonderful experiences of Afterlife. 'Don't think of those who
are slain in God's way as dead. No, they are alive,
finding their sustenance in the Presence of their Lord.
They rejoice in the bounty provided by God; and with
regard to those left behind, who have not yet joined
them, they (should) glory in the fact that on them is no
fear, nor have they cause to grieve.' (3:169-170).

A Muslim with faith does not need to grieve over
the death of a good person. They may grieve because
they have lost them, they may miss them, perhaps
tremendously, and be so sorry to be without their
company, but at least they should realise that the
'dead' loved one is not lost, mouldering and depressed, but full of light and joy and a new dimension
of life.

When a person has faith in Allah's compassion
and the Afterlife to come, it can be of enormous help
to the mourner to bear in mind that the 'dead' one does
not suddenly cease to love or care about them. It is very
important to encourage this awareness when dealing
with someone who is being overcome and consumed
by their grief. In their grief, they should try to open
their minds a little, and see things from the point of
view of the departed one. A mother who has 'died' and

entered the world-to-come will no doubt feel very concerned and sorry for an offspring or spouse who can not cope with their grief, whose life seems to hold such agony without them. Yet no matter how much they may want to, they cannot come back. They may not be able to comfort the living mourner in any way. So the bereaved person's excess grief, if it cannot be transmuted to respectful acceptance, might actually interfere with the loved one's departed state of wellbeing.

There is a famous hadith (dealt with more fully on p. 32/3) which was taken by many early Muslims to mean that 'dead' person could actually be punished for the tears of the living. Aishah corrected this misinterpretation (See p. 39-41) but it must certainly be true that if a departed soul is aware of the excess grief of the person left behind, they might well suffer through being unable to do anything about it, or comfort them.

Some people come out of grief strengthened; others become strained, depressed, anxiety-ridden, or develop psychosomatic symptoms. Only one thing is for sure—everyone who has been affected by grief can never be the same again.

If only we could all be saints, and have perfect faith in Allah! The Compassionate One wishes us all to have faith and confidence and hope. Some people do indeed find healing forces in their grief, but how can Islam help those who end up as clients of the social and health services?

A person's first response to the death of someone

who has been important to them is often shock, and
that shock is particularly pronounced when it is a
sudden unexpected death. Shock affects people in
many different ways. It may find expression in physical collapse, violent outbursts, or dazed withdrawal,
denial, and inability to take in the reality of what has
happened.

Mourners often complain that they were not prepared for what it would be like—'Why did nobody
warn me that I would feel so sick...or tired...or exhausted? Or that grief felt so like fear?' In fact, grief is
one of those things that cannot be taught by the book,
but which only makes sense after the experience.

Since bereavement is so upsetting, and the symptoms so traumatic, it may comfort mourners enor-
mously to know that certain symptoms and feelings
are almost universal responses to grief and loss, and
they are not sinful. Muslims are not only entitled to
have and express these feelings, but it would be wrong
and perhaps harmful for them to try to suppress them.
They need not fear they are lacking faith in Allah. If
they love Allah, He will open their hearts and comfort
them even while they are in their grief.

> 'O believers! Seek help with patient persever-
> ance and prayer, for God is with those who
> patiently persevere. Do not say of those who
> are slain in the way of Allah: 'They are dead'.
> No, they are living, although you may not
> perceive it.' (2:153-154).

People in the shock of bereavement are often
numbed and apathetic. Two of the best methods of

treatment are rest and warmth, yet so often those around them are impatient, and push them to 'keep going' and 'get busy', as if the important thing was to put the grief right out of their minds. This is no doubt meant kindly, but it is no real remedy, and could actually be harmful if it suppresses something that will have to surface later. It sets the scene for denial of loss and pain. Moreover, it is quite possible that the people who 'hurry' mourners into getting busy are not just concerned for the mourners, but are really only expressing their own fear or unwillingness to become involved in the mourner's pain. A grieving person may be an encumbrance, an embarrassment, or distasteful to others. The impatient helper's desire is not only to cheer up the mourners, but to get things 'back to normal' as soon as possible.

Muslims should temper their sorrow at losing a loved one with Islamic acceptance of God's will, but all mourners need to be realistic about their feelings, and not suppress them or regard them as sinful. They need to work through their grief as the Prophet himself did when he lost his beloved Khadijah and his own children, so that they may in due course reinvest their energy in new life and relationships. The loss has to be recognised, the various emotions of grief have to be released, new skills may need to be developed, and emotional energy channeled into new life.

In the first shock of the loss, the bereaved person is numb and does not feel able to bear or accept the reality of the loss. The mourner might experience a kind of mental blockage, even a denying that the loss has occurred at all. One could perhaps place the immediate reaction of the Prophet's friend Umar Ibn Al-Khattab when told of the Prophet's death into this category. It took the gentle words of Abu Bakr, and the reminder of the Qur'anic ayats revealed after the losses of Badr, to calm him and restore his good sense. 'Muhammad is no more that a Messenger; many were the messengers who passed away before him. If he dies or is slain, would you then turn back?' (3:144).

Mourners frequently find their natural grief interrupted by outbursts of anger and/or distress. Denial can sometimes take the form of manic activity—either clinging on to every memory and belonging of the deceased, or the opposite, flushing out every possible trace of them.

When a person has a powerful faith in Allah and the life to come, this sense of numbness and denial is, of course, sharply reduced. The believer with firm faith in the Afterlife mourns the loss of that loved one, maybe to a terrible degree, but does not view the death of that loved one as the end of that person. In fact, the Muslim firmly believes that the loved one has *not* ceased to exist. The 'dead' in a sense are even *more* alive than the living. Allah has taught us that this earthly life, which seems all important to us while we are here, is actually only of short duration and is not our real life at all; it is but the preparation for the real thing.

'O my people! This life of the present is nothing but (temporary) convenience; it is the

Hereafter that is the Home that will last.'
(40:39).

What a difference of emphasis, between believer and non-believer! The non-believer feels that death is the end, and therefore needs to be resisted as much as possible—for once the heart stops, that's it. One of the hardest aspects of atheistic existentialism that non-believers must cope with is the ultimate pointlessness of existence. What was it all for? What did it achieve? The older one gets the harder this is to contemplate. Believers come at it from a completely different angle. They understand and accept that no person is granted permanent life on this earth: 'We did not grant permanent life to any person before you.' (21:34). They have been granted the insight that human life is seen from the 'other side'·as just passing in a flash, or as part of a day: 'He will say: 'What number of days did you stay on earth?' They will say: 'We stayed a day, or part of a day. Yet ask those who keep account!' (23:112-113).

The 'dead' go to an afterlife prepared in advance for them. True, they will have to face judgement, and the searing light of Allah cast over all the things they did or did not do in their lives; but Muslims who have made genuine effort can face death in the confidence that they have tried to please God. They can be content that they lived in accordance to His wishes as they understood them as far as possible. Allah will overlook nothing. He will not miss our efforts, 'On that Day will people proceed in companies sorted out, to be shown the deeds that they have done; then shall everyone who has done an atom's weight of good see it, and anyone who has done an atom's weight of evil shall see it!' (99:6-8).

They may also be confident that the Lord will not consign them to Hell but will have mercy on any weaknesses they did have, failures, and sins they committed, *so long as they lived according to a good intention and were penitent for any wrongdoings they were aware of.*

> 'If you but turn against the worst of the things which you are forbidden to do, We shall expel out of you all the evil in you, and admit you to a Gate of great honour.' (4:31).

> 'Any that (in this life) has repented, believed, and worked righteousness, will have hopes to be among those who achieve salvation.' (28:67).

Allah is compassionate and full of grace and mercy. This is good news for us! Every person is weak and sinful in some way, but we need not indulge in paranoid tears or superstitious precautionery practices. Allah has told us that sinners will be punished 'except those who repent and make amends and openly declare (the Truth): to them I turn, for I am Oft-Returning, Most Merciful.' (2:160).

After a death come the days when arrangements have to be made, and the funeral faced and endured. In Islam it is recommended that the burial should take place as swiftly as possible, once death is certain. (See p. 145). In this period, the mourner is usually surrounded and supported by relatives and friends.

The presence and sympathy of others, and the 'special' position in which the mourners find themselves, cocoons them to a certain extent in a sense of 'safety'. At this early stage, even though Muslims have believed in *akhirah* (life after death) from birth, their sorrow is understood and they are expected to give vent to their grief, and to need support.[1] They are surrounded by sympathetic helpers, hopefully, and everything happens so fast. They may literally feel that they are just watching events hapen, and that their helpers will see to it that things do not get out of control, that life will go on.

The real pain and misery make themselves felt when this controlled period, and the 'privileges' that go with it, are over. The friends and helpers depart, and then the task of coming to terms with life without that loved one really begins. It is then that the mourner can really feel lost and abandoned, and develop defences against the agonies of pain.

A second very common phase in mourning, which usually starts after the friends and relatives have withdrawn and the bereaved is trying to cope again, is that of yearning and searching for the lost person. They weep and 'call' for the deceased loved one, unable to accept what their 'comforters' tell them, that the loved one has 'gone'. This may go on for a long time, for years. It is not sinful. We have the example of

---

1. See examples given on p. 34-36.

the Prophet ﷺ himself. When he was a middle-aged adult, the Prophet ﷺ once wept so copiously at the graveside of his mother (who died when he was only six), that all his companions were also moved to tears. (Abu Dawud 3228).

Sometimes the bereaved 'see' the lost person in the street or around the house; they 'see' them in un-guarded moments, in hallucinations, in dreams. They 'feel' lost spouses beside them in the bed, they smell the drift of perfume, or of tobacco. Many mourners visit places where they spent time together with the dead loved one. While in this phase, the mourner feels restless, unable to concentrate, and insomnia is very common. Again, there may be outbursts of anger or distress, restless behaviour, tension, and loss of inter-est in all that does not concern the deceased.

These symptoms lessen bit by bit as the bereaved person slowly accepts the reality of loss—but it is doubtful if the impulse to search ever completely disappears when the lost one is dearly loved. Nor are they helped by people ridiculing or belittling their experiences.

Once again, Islam comes to aid the grieving soul. The state of departed souls is a mystery known only to God; but there is a strong tradition that the tranquillising notion of the dead 'resting in peace' or 'sleeping' in their graves until Judgement Day is just wishful thing, and is not actually what happens. Muslim tradition suggests that the souls of good people will be able to range far and wide, having all sorts of experiences.

These may all relate to their new state of life, but who could deny that perhaps these souls might well wish to console their mourners, and might be granted the opportunity, if God wills, to visit them with their loving presence?

Therefore, if it is God's will for the departed loved ones to be 'felt' by the griever as a comforting presence, then God knows best, and no-one will be able to deny this close feeling. Many Muslims feel very aware of the loving good wishes of their dear departed, consoling them in their natural loss. Muslims take courage, and recognise that the departed are *not* lost, but if God wills, are safe on the next stage of their journey.

The Prophet prayed: 'O Allah, forgive (this our dead loved one), lift him up to the company of those who have followed Your path in righteousness; let him become a guide and helper to (us) his descendants who survive him. O Lord of the universe, make his grave spacious, and grant him light in it.' (Muslim 2003).

Since the awareness of after-life is so strongly felt, the pain of grief is not one of irrevocable loss but only the pangs of being parted for a while. The Prophet ﷺ used to visit the graves of those he loved regularly, and sit beside them thinking about them and praying for them. (See p. 35, 36, 152).

Another phase commonly encountered in mourning is the heartbreaking physical sense of disorganisation and despair. This is probably the most painful part of the experience for non-believers, when

they begin slowly to change from protest to resignation, and accept that the loss is final for the rest of their
time on earth. The dead loved one is never going to
return, and no matter how much they might like leave
this earth and 'go with them' it is not God's will, and
they must start life afresh without that person.

This acceptance can only happen when the bereaved person feels strong enough to bear this knowledge. In fact, the denial, pretence and numbing of
feeling that characterise the first phases are necessary
defences against pain that cannot yet be borne.

The Muslim encounters all these natural feelings,
just like a non-believer, and tries to cope with them. It
is, of course, quite devastating when a loved one
passes on, but the true Muslim regards it as a duty to
accept whatever will God has for their lives, even if
they cannot understand the reason for their suffering
and loss. They know that all humans are mortal, and
the times of their deaths were known by Allah from the
moment they were conceived. They draw consolation
from the knowledge that the 'dead' person is not really
dead at all, but is in another place, experiencing other
things; and that how they react to that person's loss is
a very real part of their test of life.

If God wills, the loss of someone we love will not
be final at all, but there will come a time when we will
be re-united. This is not speculation for a Muslim for
it is clearly stated in the Qur'an.

> 'For those who patiently persevere.... there is
> the final attainment of the (Eternal) Home—

Gardens of perpetual bliss; they shall enter there, as well as the righteous among their fore-fathers (male and female), their spouses and their offspring.' (13:22-23).

'And those who believe and whose families follow them in faith—to them shall we join their families, nor shall we deprive them of their works.' (52:21).

Until that time, it is our duty to bear the pain patiently, and not let our grief become a cause of concern for the 'dead' loved one!

If we really care for the dead loved one, it should console us to realise that although the time may seem long to us, for the dead loved ones it will pass in a flash:

'Take the similitude of one who passed by a hamlet all in ruins, saying 'Oh! How shall God ever bring it to life after this death?' But God caused him to die for a hundred years, then raised him up again. He said: 'How long did you remain (in that state of death)? 'He said perhaps a day, or part of a day.' God said: 'No, you remained in that condition a hundred years; but look at your food and drink— they show no signs of ageing; and look at your donkey; and that We may make of you a sign for the people, look further at the bones, how We bring them together and clothe them with flesh.' When this was shown clearly to him, he said: 'I know now that God has power over all things.' (2:259).

'One day He will gather them together; (it will be) as if they had tarried but an hour of the day; they will recognise each other.' (10:45).

Muslims know their own lives are gifts from Allah. It is the highest act of submission to give this life back to Him without argument, resistance or complaint; even to give it eagerly, when called for. If a Muslim lives every day in service of God, to their best ability, then it is not so difficult to accept God's call when it comes, and reply humbly—'I am ready. At Your command, O Lord.'

There are several hadith which reveal the personal bereavements of the Prophet Muhammad ﷺ, and those of close friends of his, which give an excellent indication of the true believer's reaction to the death of much-loved ones. A natural grief was accepted as the sign of compassion, but the true Muslim also accepted that the life was God's gift, which God could take back as He chose.

One incident referred to the death of one of the Apostle's ﷺ grandsons, the son of his daughter Zaynab.

Usamah ibn Zayd reported: 'While we were with the Apostle of Allah ﷺ one of his daughters sent to him to call him and inform him that her son was dying. The Messenger of Allah ﷺ told the messenger to go back and tell her that what Allah had taken belonged to Him, and to Him belonged what He granted; and (since) everything happened according to His appointed time, so he requested her to show endurance and seek reward from Allah. The messenger came back and said: She begs you to come to her. He got up to go, accompanied by Sa'd ibn Ubadah, Mu'adh ibn Jabal, and I also went along with them. The child was lifted to him, and his soul was feeling restless as if it was in an old (waterskin). The Prophet's ﷺ eyes welled up with tears. Sa'd said: 'What is this, Messenger of Allah?' He replied: 'This is compassion which Allah has placed in the hearts of His servants; and God shows compassion only to those of His servants who are compassionate.' (Muslim 2008; the same hadith is reported in Abu Dawud 3119 with slight variations).

When the Prophet's ﷺ own son, Ibrahim, died, once again the Prophet ﷺ did not withold from weeping.

Anas ibn Malik reported that : 'I saw (the baby Ibrahim) at the point of death, before the Apostle of Allah ﷺ. Tears began to fall from the eyes of the Apostle of Allah ﷺ. He said: 'The eye weeps and the heart grieves, but we say only what our Lord is pleased with, and we are grieved for you, O Ibrahim.' (Abu Dawud 3120).

The Prophet's ﷺ friend, Umm Sulaym, showed admirable faith and endurance when her little son died. She asked the members of her family not to tell Abu Talhah (the father) until she had spoken to him first. When he came home, she gave him his supper, and made herself attractive, and even satisfied his sexual hunger. Then, when she saw that he was satisfied in every respect, she said to him: 'Abu Talhah, if some people borrow something from another family and then they ask for its return, should they resist its return? 'He said: 'No.' She said: '(Then) I tell you about the death of your son.' Abu Talhah was actually annoyed that she had not told him before, and went to report everything to the Prophet ﷺ, but he said: 'May Allah bless both of you in the night spent by you.' It so happened that she became pregnant that night, and they were blessed with a new baby. (Adapted from Muslim 6013; see also Muslim 5341).

All too frequently a grieving person develops symptoms that are treated with tranquillisers and anti-depressants, but this is only covering up the pains that are hurting, a temporary relief and one, moreover, that may be building up more problems for the future if the patient becomes dependent on those drugs.

The last phase of mourning may come a long time later, depending on one's faith and fortitude. Eventually the bereaved really will relinquish their lost ones, and begin to face up to and adapt to everyday life again without them, and without a compulsive clinging on to every little memory. Only after the mourners have lived with their loss and, perhaps, built up the beginnings of a new life, are they really accepting the finality of the loss.

Mourning is not an illness, or anything to be ashamed of—it is the cure to the grief.

The most vital and useful part of that mourning is the faith of the bereaved person, their Islam. Muslims know it is a waste of time fretting or worrying over what will happen, or trying to prolong lives or shorten them contrary to the will of God. Ultimately, everything is in His hands, and His care is over all.

'If you think that you control your own desti-
nies, then try to stop your souls leaving your
bodies at the time of your death.' (3:168, 56:83-
87).

'Say: I have no power over any harm or profit
to myself except as Allah wills. To every
people is a term appointed: when their term is
reached, not one hour can they cause delay,
nor can they advance it.' (10:49).

'Nor can a soul die except by God's leave, the
term being fixed as by writing.' (3:149).

The Prophet ﷺ expressed the perfect attitude
towards accepting the end of our unknown timespans
on earth: 'At evening, do not expect to live till morning;
at morning, do not expect to live till evening. Take from
your health for your illness, and from your life for your
death.' (Muslim).

Strong faith and Islam give us the patience to bear
the losses, to control the yearning for loved ones who
have been taken from us, and temper it with the desire
to accept God's will gracefully and with resignation.
As Muslims, we should hope to pass through our time
of mourning with dignity and true acknowledgement
of reality, and to turn our eyes forward to new life—
one of doing His will with hopes unshaken.

Chapter 3

The Importance of Weeping

How can one be of help to the person who is in mourn-ing? The kind of help really needed is what is known as 'crisis and grief therapy', a process of help designed to mobilise the mourner's healthy forces when the grief process is being blocked or is in danger of turning pathological. If the bereaved person is a Muslim of good faith, then the task is made that much easier, because certain factors will be taken for granted. Nevertheless, human beings are human, and the pains of a spouse grieving for a lost partner, or a parent for a lost child, or child for a lost parent, are excruciating whatever the faith of the mourner.

Muslims believe that human life is a gift of God, which He gives and takes away as He chooses. It is the duty of the believer to accept his or her allotted time, and be prepared to hand the soul back to Allah with patience and readiness at the appropriate moment. 'To Him we belong, and to Him we return' (2:156,28:70, 96:8) is a passage quoted frequently.

Therefore it is taken to be a lack of faith if a person is oppressed by too much grief, for this means that they have not accepted the will of God in their hearts but are resisting it. However, it is no help whatsoever to 'nag'

the grieving person, or adopt a sanctimonious attitude—one which reproaches them if their faith seems
to be wavering, or if, in the opinion of the 'helper', their
grief is accused of being wrong because it seems to
deny their genuine belief and trust in God.

The most valuable healing ability for any human
being is the ability to shed tears, so it is therefore very
helpful if the bereaved person is able to give way to
this expression of sorrow. If the mourner is 'bottled up'
or 'pressed down', the crisis-helper might perhaps
choose a suitable moment in which to say something
that will release those healing floods which bring relief
to the soul.

Tears are not forbidden in Islam; in fact, they are
very important to unblock the shock and numbness
that grips the mourner. By the grace of Allah, in the
tears are forces that heal both physically and mentally.
Tears have a relieving effect on the stress produced by
loss and trauma. They really are a gift from Allah—it
is an important sign for us that humans are the only
animals that react to stress in this way. Our tears were
maybe specially created by Allah for us human beings,
to serve a useful purpose.

It is therefore important to remember that it is
harmful when mourners are told that weeping is weak
or babyish, or that their loss is 'nothing to cry about.'
(Incidentally, one has to be careful when encouraging
children not to cry, too. The person's ability to grieve
in later life could be impaired if they think weeping is
always babyish, and as an adult, he or she might be

unable to resolve the stresses in a natural and whole-some way. Some children gradually learn to control themselves so tightly that as adults they never weep).

The weeping designed by Allah to heal is the profound sobbing in which the tensions of the body are let go. The tensions arise from the muscles of the body contracting as a defence against both physical and mental pain, so that the pain does not become too overwhelming for the body's autonomic nervous system. This weeping may also unleash chronic tensions which derive from any old unprocessed traumas lingering from the past. Tears probably also restore the body's natural balance in connection with stress. Investigations show that the chemical content of the tears in weeping is different from that of the tears from eyes that are merely 'watering'.

How can you help a weeping person? Should you ignore them, or try to stop them? Or encourage them to 'let it all flow'? When a person is weeping, some appreciate body contact and others do not. The befriender could try putting arms around the mourner—it is a simple matter, and you can easily judge whether it is appreciated or not. Some people are comforted by this, others stiffen and become insecure. If in doubt, ask if they wish it. Sometimes it is precisely this body contact of a friend that gives the necessary courage to 'let go'.

The Blessed Prophet ﷺ did not object to this normal and natural weeping, and indeed, as we have seen, he wept himself on many occasions. He suffered many close bereavements, and knew for himself the dreadful pains of grief and loss. He never knew his father (who died before he was born); he lost his mother when he was only six years old and his beloved grandfather when he was eight. Khadijah bore him two sons who died in infancy. He lost Khadijah, his wife and chief supporter for twenty-five years. In his later years, he lost another wife, Zaynab bint Khuzaymah (the widow of his friend Ubaydah), a lady who had been very much loved for her sweetness and generosity. Then three of his four daughters (who grew up and married) died before he did, and so did several of the grandchildren he adored. Needless to say, in a lifetime that included a considerable amount of warfare, he also lost many dearly-loved friends. Finally, his son Ibrahim (born when the Prophet 鷺 was quite an old man) died when he was around six months old.

Numerous moving hadiths record the reaction of the Prophet 鷺 to the deaths of people he loved:

Anas ibn Malik recorded: 'We went with Allah's Messenger 鷺 to the blacksmith Abu Saif, and he was the husband of the wet-nurse of Ibrahim. Allah's Messenger 鷺 picked Ibrahim up and kissed him, and smelled him; later we went back to Abu Saif's house and this time Ibrahim was drawing his last breaths. The eyes of the Messenger of Allah 鷺 started shedding tears. Abdur Rahman ibn Auf said: 'O Allah's Apostle 鷺, even you are weeping!' He replied: 'O Ibn Auf, this is compassion.' Then he wept more and said: 'The eyes are shedding tears and the heart is grieved, yet we will

AIN

THE IMPORTANCE OF WEEPING 41

not speak except what pleases our Lord. O Ibrahim! Truly we are grieved by your being separated (from us).' (Bukhari 23.42.390; Muslim 5733; Abu Dawud 3120).

Aishah recorded: ' I saw the Apostle of Allah ﷺ kiss (his friend) Uthman ibn Mazun when he died, and I saw that tears were flowing from his eyes (Abu Dawud 3157).

When his friend Sa'd ibn Ubadah died, the Blessed Prophet ﷺ spoke up to reassure those who felt that shedding tears was wrong, but who could not help doing so:

Abdullah ibn 'Umar recorded that Sa'd ibn Ubadah complained of illness. The Messenger of Allah ﷺ came to visit him, accompanied by Abdur Rahman ibn Auf, Sa'd ibn Abi Waqqas, and Abdullah ibn Masud. As he entered (his room) he found he had fainted away. He said: 'Has he died?' They said: 'Messenger of Allah ﷺ, it is not so.' The Messenger of Allah ﷺ wept. When the people saw Allah's Messenger ﷺ weeping, they also began to weep. He said: 'Listen; Allah does not punish anyone for the tears that the eye sheds or the grief that the heart feels; but He punishes for this (pointing to his tongue), or He shows mercy.' (Muslim 2010).

Abu Hurayrah recorded that even many years after the death of his mother, the Blessed Prophet ﷺ used to visit her grave and his weeping over her caused all those with him to weep also. The hadith recorded that he asked permission to pray for forgiveness for her, but this was not allowed. Even the mother of the Prophet 鏴 himself could not be granted any kind of preferential treatment; at the judgement each person is judged solely upon their own record, and one person is quite powerless to plead for another. However, he was granted permission to visit her grave, and he encouraged Muslims to 'visit graves—for they make you remember death.' (Abu Dawud 3228; hadith 3229 mentioned a previous ban on visiting graves which was now rescinded).

Aishah recorded that the Messenger 鏴 sometimes even left his bed at night, and went to sit sadly beside his dead loved ones in the cemetery of Baqi. (See p. 152).

It is therefore very clear that the Prophet 鏴 did not disapprove of weeping, or a person's natural grief. Tears are a sign of genuine love and sorrow at the temporary parting. They are not a sign of weakness but of love. It was the raising of loud and ostentatious wailing such as the professional mourners used to do, that was strictly forbidden in Islam.

Usayd ibn Abu Usayd recorded on the authority of one of the Muslim women who swore the oath to the Prophet 鏴 that: 'One of the oaths which the Apostle of Allah 鏴 received from us about virtue was... that we would not scratch the face, nor wail, nor tear the front of our garments nor dishevel the hair.' (Abu Dawud 3125).

Abdullah recorded: 'He who slaps his cheeks, tears his clothes and follows the ways and traditions of the days of jahiliyyah (ignorance) is not one of us.'

(Bukhari 23.34.382).

The Prophet 🕌 disliked these histrionics, for no matter what the grief of the mourners, Muslims should trust in Allah that their dead loved ones (who died in faith) would be finding peace and happiness, released from their sufferings, in a better place; and that they themselves would be able to survive the pain and grief and loss, and pick up the threads of their lives, helped by their own faith.

Umm Salamah (the widow of the Prophet's 🕌 cousin, who later married the Prophet 🕌 herself) recorded: 'When Abu Salamah died, I said: 'I am a stranger in a strange land; I shall weep for him in a manner that will be talked of.' I made preparation for weeping for him, and a woman from the upper side of the city came there who intended to help me (in weeping). She happened to come across the Prophet 🕌 and he said: 'Do you intend to bring the devil back into a house from which Allah has twice driven him out?' I therefore refrained from weeping, and I did not weep.' (Muslim 2007). She was obviously talking about the traditional loud, public grieving done in honour of the dead.

Mourners should bear themselves patiently, in faith and hope, believing that their loved ones will, if God wills, be pardoned by Allah for any sins and shortcomings, and hoping they will be received by the angels into the next world with love and welcome.

On the other hand, there is no need for a mourner to feel guilty if they did not weep. Some mourners might think they had omitted something, and had not treated the corpse with proper respect and deep feeling if they had not wept. Some people even feel guilty for not weeping when they had not realised their loved one had died, or were not in possession of the knowledge of the demise. They foolishly wonder if they are guilty of omission, or if the soul of the deceased might have been grieved by it.

The following hadith suggests that no mourner need feel guilty whether they weep over the dead or not; whatever their reaction, God's angels are already taking care of the soul of the deceased:

Jabir ibn Abdullah recorded: 'When my father was martyred, I lifted the sheet from his face and wept; and the people forbade me to do so, but the Prophet 鸞 did not forbid me. Then my aunt Fatimah began weeping, and the Prophet 鸞 said: 'It makes no difference (to him) whether you weep or not. The angels were shading him all the time with their wings until you (came and) carried him from the field.' (Bukhari 23.3.336).

Real grief should not be for these ones, but for those who failed in their tests of life, and deserted faith in God. These cases are the real tragedies, for their fates will be unpleasant in the extreme, and no amount of grieving and pleading will be able to alter their lot.

In normal cases, Muslims are urged to show faith and fortitude:

Anas ibn Malik recorded that Allah's Messenger 鸞 came to a woman who had been weeping for her child, (other hadiths state that she was sitting by the side of his grave) and said to her: 'Fear Allah, and show endurance.' She, (not recognising him) said: 'You have not been afflicted as I have been!' When he had gone, they told her it was the Messenger of Allah ﷺ. She was embarrassed and shocked, and came to his door, and she did not find any doorkeepers at his door. She said: 'Messenger of Allah, I did not recognise you.' He said: 'Endurance is to be shown at the first blow.' (Muslim 2013).

So, weeping is condoned, but excessive grief shows lack of faith in Allah. Certainly the practices from the time of jahiliyyah are strongly disapproved—where mourners made a mighty drama out of noisy weeping and wailing, as if the more noisy and public the grief the more is demonstrated that the dead person was loved and respected. Without Islam, of course, these mourners believed their dead really were dead, with no hope of a life to come.

For example, when the Prophet's ﷺ friend Abu Musa died, he felt it necessary to rebuke his wife for her wailing. His son Abu Burda recorded that 'he (Abu Musa) was afflicted with grave pain and he fell unconscious, with his head in the lap of a lady of his household. One of the women of his household (his wife Umm Abdullah) wailed. He was unable (because of his weakness) to say anything to her, but when he rallied a little, he said....'Truly, the Messenger of Allah ﷺ has no concern with the woman who wails loudly, shaves her hair or tears her garments.' (Muslim 186,187;

Abu Dawud 3124 for Yazid ibn Aws' version).

It is important to make the difference between true grief and ostentatious wailing, the ancient custom showing respect for the dead. This must be quite clear, because controversy about weeping arose in the earliest of times as the result of one of the hadiths of the Prophet's friend and successor Umar.

Abdullah ibn 'Umar recorded that his sister Hafsah (who had become the Prophet's fourth wife) wept for (their father) 'Umar (when he was about to die). 'Umar said: 'Be quiet, my daughter. Don't you know that the Messenger of Allah ﷺ said that the dead are punished because of the family's weeping over him?' (Muslim 2015).

His friend Suhaib, who was at the deathbed, also wept and was rebuked. Abu Musa recorded that Suhaib had gone to Umar's house when he heard Umar was wounded (by an assassin), and stood by his side and began to wail. Upon this Umar said: 'What are you weeping for? Are you weeping for me?' He said: 'By Allah, it is for you that I weep, O commander of the believers.' He said: 'By Allah, you already know that the Messenger of Allah ﷺ said: 'He who is lamented is punished.' (Muslim 2020).

These hadiths were the subject of much heated discussion and incidentally, they show the importance of very careful hadith study—for they run in direct contradiction to the word of the Qur'an that 'No bearer of a burden shall bear the burden of another.' (6:134). It is therefore inconceivable that the Merciful Allah would punish a dead person for the faults of his family! This was the point of view argued by Aishah and Ibn Abbas, among others.

When Abu Musa reported the saying to Musa ibn Talhah, he told him that Aishah had said it was something concerning the Jews. When Abdullah ibn Abu Mulaika went to Aishah and told her what Umar had said; she exclaimed:

'May Allah have mercy upon Umar! I swear by Allah that Allah's Messenger ﷺ never said that the dead would be punished because of his family's lamenting for him. Truly, it is Allah Who has caused (both) laughter and weeping. No bearer of a burden will bear another's burden.' (Muslim 2022).

Ibn Abu Mulaika recorded that al-Qasim ibn Muhammad commented that when the words of Umar and Ibn Umar were conveyed to Aishah, she said tactfully: 'You have (indeed) narrated it to me from those who are neither liars nor suspected of lying, but sometimes hearing misleads.' (Muslim 2022).

Amra bint Abd al-Rahman recorded that she heard Aishah make a mention to her about Abdullah ibn Umar saying 'the dead is punished because of the lamentation of the living.' Upon this, Aishah said: 'May Allah have mercy upon the father of Abd al-Rahman (i.e. Ibn Umar). He did not tell a lie, but he forgot, or made a mistake. The Messenger of Allah ﷺ happened to pass by a dead Jewess who was being mourned over. Upon this, he remarked: 'They weep over her, and she is being punished in the grave.'

(Muslim 2029).

Another hadith suggests a variant interpretation—
that part of the punishment given to deceased unbelievers would be because of the sorrow and suffering
they had caused their families:

Ibn Abbas recorded that when Umar died he made
mention about it to Aishah. She said: 'May Allah have
mercy upon Umar! I swear by Allah that Allah's
Messenger ﷺ never said that Allah would punish the
believer because of the weeping, but he said that Allah
would increase the punishment of an unbeliever because of the weeping of his family over him.' (Muslim
2023). In other words, his unbelieving conduct will
have caused suffering to his family and increased their
grief, and he would be held to account for it.

The dead person is not responsible for what others
do to express their grief. In other words, if a man's
female relatives wail after they realise he is dead, he is
certainly not punished for what they do—it is they
who bear the responsibility for their actions.

It is important that Muslims accept what Allah has
willed with resignation and submission. Wailing is not
a mark of submission to Allah's will—if anything, it is
more of a protest. Far better to praise Allah for the
achievements of that person's life, and pray that the
deceased will be forgiven their shortcomings and
accepted into Heaven.

Several prayers of the Prophet have been recorded, and serve as excellent examples for us. Some
may even sound slightly odd or even selfish to the

modern ear, but they remind us that our loved one has gone to his or her Eternal Home, and we should compose ourselves, console ourselves for the loss of a friend or relative, and accept the comfort and closeness of friends and relatives who are still with us, or whom we have yet to meet:

'To Allah we belong and to Him we return. My Lord, reward me for my tragedy and compensate me with better than I have lost.' (Ahmad and Muslim).

You cannot force a person to stop grieving , any more than you can force a person to fall in love, or believe in God in the first place. It is worse than misguided when an over-pious person actually adds to the mourner's grief and pain by harping on their apparent weakness, and reprimands them—usually from the stance of moral superiority.

Our dear Allah understands the mourner's loss perfectly well—and the Blessed Apostle ﷺ, while having the most perfect faith in Allah and the life to come—was nevertheless able to comfort the bereaved with great sympathy.

How can we help them? Firstly, by remembering our Lord's gracious promise and believing it—'On no soul do I place a burden greater than it can bear!' (2:286; 23:62).

This is the most wonderful consolation, and bringer of hope. Even when we are so bowed down that we do not know how to cope or carry on, God is with us—on the darkest night, in the wildest storm, in our deepest despair. He knows our suffering, and will be with us through all our period of panic. (2:177). If we stand firm, confident of that love and those promises, then our pains will not destroy us.

Chapter 4

Giving Help to the Grief-Stricken

Crisis help is the giving of emotional 'first aid' when the loss or the traumatic experience is so overwhelming that the grievers are in danger of being submerged by their emotions.

The most basic help of all is to realise that every mourner should have somebody to stand alongside them, so that they do not grieve alone. Help can be quite simple, and physical—a hot drink, a blanket, an affectionate arm or hand; little touches like these make all the difference in the world.

Abd Allah ibn Jafar recorded the Prophet's ﷺ recommendation that when visiting bereaved families it was a kindness to prepare food and take it with you, so as not to be a burden to the mourners (Abu Dawud 3126). It is hardly a kindness for sympathisers to turn up in droves and expect mourners to wait on them hand and foot, or even really to provide food for them at all—that could turn into an enormous burden. If such a thing is likely to happen, because of a mourner's particular culture, it would be a real kindness to take the support of some helper, perhaps a relative not so involved, or friend or neighbour, to make the drinks and offer refreshments.

How do the mourners feel? They feel overwhelmed by pain, tears, and very frequently a mixture of guilt, anger and fear. They have difficulty in sleeping, their hearts palpitate, they suffer indigestion, stomach disorders, body aches—in fact, their whole nervous system has been disturbed.

These mourning symptoms are not just confined to losing loved people, incidentally. They can also occur when people have lost other things to which they were closely attached, such as career, job, money, prestige, home, land and other possessions. Divorce, or a husband insisting on taking another wife although the first wife is terribly hurt by this, and retirement from a loved and fulfilling job, especially premature retirement through redundancy, can be devastating. Things like being the victim of theft or fraud or cheating, and losing special items of jewellery, or inherited land and homes, or being 'reduced' from being a famous and rich person to a pauper and nonentity, are equally traumatic.

Appearance and health are two other powerful 'attachments'—if someone loses a breast or a hand, arm, leg or eye, or becomes badly disfigured by accident, disease or fire, and loses their pleasant looks— all these losses trigger off mourning symptoms, and need 'healing'. Women who have been beautiful in their youth may have great grief when coping with increasing fatness, and the sags and wrinkles of old age.

Psychologically, people who have previously had

difficulty in their attachment process towards other people or things may also have problems in living through fresh emotions of grief in a healing way. When facing bereavement, if there have been any past experiences of loss, grief and abandonment, the memories and emotions all rush to the surface again, and old wounds—even memories from as long ago as early childhood—can be re-opened.

However, there is also the possibility of good coming out of this, too. If a person has a 'skeleton in the cupboard', something which happened in the past for which grief was never completed, the new occasion for grief can actually open the floodgates that damned up that past trauma, and good can result—the healing for both can take place.

Grief is not a disease, but if incorrectly handled it can easily develop into one. It is not in itself sinful, but if clung on to it blocks the healing powers of faith, and room is given for the devil to take over. Suffering can sometimes be a powerful motivator towards insight and goodness; but if wrongly handled it can also alter people's characters in sinister and life-destroying ways. It is quite possible to die of a 'broken heart' and sober factual research shows clearly that mortality increases by an enormous per cent in widows and widowers.

We have to accept that the loss is a reality that our sick loved one, who has perhaps been ill for a long time, is dead. Every day some 200,000 people die—by disease, mischance, murder, starvation, war, natural catastrophe. Some die whilst still in the womb, others from old age. Some die at peace with the world, others fighting all the way.

The bereaved person must face up to the recognition that their loss is irrevocable. This is sometimes achieved quite easily when the beloved one has been 'released' after a long and painful illness, but it can be more difficult to accept in cases of sudden or violent death.

If the deceased was loved, respected and cherished, it takes a long time to sink in that they have gone for ever from this earth—that perhaps for years the mourner will never again see the loved one, hear the well-known voice, feel their loving arms or kiss. A bereaved partner has to accept that they no longer have a future together.

The death may mean that we have to live without the comfort of bodily warmth in our beds at night, and sexual feelings may have to be suppressed if we have become 'half a couple'. At first, the pain will grow, because the recognition that the loss is irrevocable will slowly become plainer. The mourner will have to change his/her life, and learn new skills, and ask for help in different ways from before. Only eventually will the mourner learn to invest energy in new ways, which shows they are reconciled to their grief.

Some people, especially men, suppress their grief—they feel that they must not let it show, not in front of the children, or in front of their religious friends. It is important to them that life must go on, that they show their faith to be genuine—as if God anywhere required us not to grieve for our loved ones! If they are suppressing their grief, these people may become restless, maybe even hyperactive. They are not getting rid of the problem, merely putting it aside for a while. Months or years later a sad film, or sympathetic shoulder, or anything, will trigger off and reopen all this suppressed grief, and they will be obliged to face it after all.

If grief is not fully expressed and worked through, all sorts of psychosomatic symptoms occur—vague pains for which an organic cause cannot be found; actual ailments like peptic ulcers, heart conditions, asthma, headaches, etc. Sometimes the bereaved develop symptoms that closely resemble those of the deceased.

There are psychological symptoms too—sadness, emptiness, anxiety, vehement self-reproach, guilt. Some develop a strong dependence on others, or alternatively a total isolation and cutting off. They display phobic behaviour towards things that belonged to the deceased—either stripping the house of all reminders, or keeping a bedroom as a shrine.

Healthy grief is flexible, pathological grief is more rigid. It is normal and polite to leave the deceased's bedroom untouched for a while after death. But what then? Does it become a shrine of memories, everything remaining untouched forever as a memorial room? In some bereaved people, thoughts about the dead person and emotions of grief replace almost everything else and go on for months if not years. These grievers almost worship everything that had to do with their loved one. Bedrooms remain untouched for years, the clothes worn by the deceased are kept hanging in the wardrobe. The mourners go to sit there to cling on to their memories.

Or, on the other hand, is there complete avoidance of the room? Is everything got rid of so fanatically that no reminders at all are left to disturb the mourner? If the bereaved person appears to have a paranoid insistence that everything has to go, that may betray an emotional rigidity which may inhibit the work of grieving—the mourner is foolishly trying to cover things over as though nothing has happened.

Sometimes a bereaved person keeps the clothes, but does everything to avoid the room associated with the lost one. Sometimes they isolate themselves so much they become bitter and unapproachable.

The Prophet 🕌 himself, although he remarried many times in the few years left to him after losing his beloved Khadijah, never forgot his love for her. It was one of the hardest things his later wife Aishah had to accept—she said once that she never felt so jealous of any of his other wives as she did of Khadijah, for he never ceased to remember her and praise her.

Once, when she spoke to the Blessed Prophet 🕌 about her own feelings, he softly rebuked her, for it was Allah Himself who had nurtured his love for Khadijah and her love for him.

There is one famous hadith that recounts the Blessed Prophet 🕌 being overcome with emotion when Khadijah's sister Halah came to visit him, and hearing her very similar voice, he thought for a moment that it was Khadijah. Aishah rebuked him:— 'Why do you remember an old woman so often, who has been dead for a long time, and Allah has given you better wives?' The Blessed Muhammad ﷺ replied—'I can never forget her! She believed in me when no-one else did; she embraced Islam when people did not accept me, and she helped and comforted me when there was none to lend me a helping hand.' (Bukhari and Muslim).

Chapter 5

Crisis Intervention and Letting Go

C ontroversy rages over whether it is better for relatives to see the corpse or not. In Islam, the ritual washing of a dead body is a *fard kifayah*, a duty incumbent upon the Muslim community. If no Muslim washes the body of a dead brother or sister-in-Islam, all the Muslims in that community incur a sin.

It is normal for the relatives of the deceased to take upon themselves the task of rendering the final washing and swathing of their loved one, and not to leave it to strangers. These last intimate services to the loved one are done with care and respect (see p. 135), and are in themselves aids towards healing grief.

Seeing the body of the deceased is an important part of the mourning process. The encounter with the stiff lifeless body makes it easier to recognise that they are gone, and to let them go. The sight of the corpse is usually quite enough to trigger off the healing reaction of grief naturally. It makes it clear beyond doubt or false hope that the farewell is inevitable.

If the body of the dead person has never been seen, as in a case of loss at sea or in a foreign country, or when the corpse has been totally destroyed, as in a bombing—it is very difficult to accept the death of that person. Maybe the missing person is still alive somewhere? The mourners cling desperately to their forlorn hopes.

The sight of the corpse usually triggers the recognition that their spirit has gone forever—the body is no more than an empty shell. The loss strikes home, and the bereaved person begins to weep. This viewing of the corpse is therefore not just a morbid curiosity; it is very important. Some people argue that they wish to keep in their minds the picture of their loved ones as they were, and not the sight of their dead corpses. However, it does seem that if the dead person is not seen, the parting is that much more difficult.

Muslims wrap their beloved dead in simple white cloths, but it is preferable if the face can be left visible until the mourners have seen it. (See p. 135 for full details of wrapping and shrouding).

There is a human need to say a final farewell, and most people feel cheated if they are deprived of this. Children should not be excluded from this farewell, either, and their grief should be taken just as seriously as that of the adults. Caring mourners should prepare children for what they will see, and perhaps hold their hands through the farewells.

Adults who lost parents as children often feel cheated if they did not see them and make final farewell. Mothers should see their stillborn babies. If they see and bury their dead babies they are well started on their work of grieving. (See p. 76).

After a death, many people have the need to recount over and over again the details of that death. Now, the helper is most valuable not for speaking, or 'finding the right words', but just for being there, and for taking the time to listen patiently.

If the reality of their loss is not accepted, it may be that crisis intervention is needed. The mourners may not take kindly to it, for they may be beset by a massive denial of reality. In these cases, the reaction tends to be—'You mustn't say that—it's too cruel!' The person helping them through their grief has the task of making them face up to their loss.

It is interesting and instructive to recall how even the Prophet's ﷺ devout and sternly self-disciplined companion Umar reacted when he heard of the death of the Prophet ﷺ. His instant reaction was to refuse to accept it—and it took the gentle tact of Abu Bakr to calm him with Allah's own words:

> 'Muhammed ﷺ is no more than a Messenger;
> many were the Messengers who passed away
> before him. If he died or were slain, would
> you then turn back on your heels?' (3:144).

The bereaved person may feel overwhelmed with despair, fear, feelings of being abandoned, loneliness, perhaps guilt and shame. Other common reactions are violent anger—against the world, against fate, against God or against the deceased themselves. You will often hear them say things like:—'How could he die and leave me?' 'I can't live without him.' 'Everything worth living for has gone.'

Hopefully, these statements are a nonsense—but it is how they feel at that stage, and that feeling is very strong and real. The true facing of reality has to come later, and—thanks be to Allah—in Islam it is made so very much easier by the acceptance of God's will and the sure knowledge that when we die our souls will be treated with justice and compassion.

Sometimes it can be useful to use a simple metaphor to help the mourner to widen their perspective on their pain. You could tell them they have a choice. They can be a chick or an egg. If they choose to be an egg, then they'll see the end of their relationship with their dead loved one as the destruction of the whole fabric of their life. It will split in half and fall into two empty shells. Alternatively, they can see themselves as the chick that comes out of the egg. In that case they will feel small, very vulnerable, greatly in need of warmth and comfort and food. Above all, they'll have the craving for security. But as a chick they will grow. A smashed eggshell never recovers.

Often the beareaved person needs someone with whom they can think aloud, and who is there while they work out their own solutions. A friend on the end of a telephone may provide just the sounding board which can enable us to face and articulate fears which might otherwise take hold of us. A friend who is willing to make a regular commitment to a bereaved person is doubly valuable—they are not only helpful, but their regular help provides much-needed stability in this uneasy time. Someone who can 'be around' for as long as the bereaved person has need of them, is a real lifeline.

The unhelpful response is to jump to conclusions and be over-anxious to protect. We can be very good at giving unwanted advice, and making simple issues more complicated. The most helpful response is probably to be still, and to accept, enabling the person to go at their own pace. Anything more than that might divest the mourner of what dignity they have left, of their ability to make their own choices, to be a growing person.

There are many factors which influence responses to bereavement, such as mode of death (how did the person die?), timeliness, previous warning, and preparation for bereavement; but the key factors seems to be genuine faith, and the relationships or interactions that existed between the surviving and the dead.

Helpers must be calm, strong and sympathetic, able to understand and empathise, a mixture of security and authority. To approach the grief-stricken person with too 'matter-of-fact' a manner is just as bad as being too sugary. A true helper can weep with the mourner, but should not have their broad view blocked—they should try to show how there are healing forces to be found in the tears and anger of the mourners, so they should not be afraid or ashamed of them. They can help to reduce fear, shame and guilt by convincing mourners that their grief is a healthy sign, and not an illness.

Some mourners develop bitterness and chronic grief and withdraw into isolation, convinced that nobody can really understand how difficult things are for them. They may feel so impoverished that they become deeply depressed and feel they cannot continue to live. They may not even want to live, because they feel that only life with the dead loved one had any value. This is very upsetting for other members of the family. For example, mothers or fathers who have lost idealised partners may so instill in their children the feeling that everything worth having belongs to the dead that they burden the children with hurt and constant self-doubts. This living with death is the very opposite from accepting death.

If such a person is not helped to resolve the anxieties which underlie these reactions, he or she will go on repressing and denying feelings—feelings of love as well as hate, those of joy as well as sorrow—and will develop into an unfeeling, unemotional person.[1] Needless to say, once they get into this state, it is very difficult for the people who care for them to keep patient, and go on loving them.

Loneliness is one of the most poignant forms of human suffering. It is a desperate feeling of separation from those who give meaning to life. The loneliness that accompanies acute grief is an assault on the meaning of life itself. It is an acute threat to the inner security system of an individual, the devastating loss

---

1. See 'Death and Family', L.Pincus, Faber 1976, p.172.

of some of the essential nature of the self.

When people truly love others they become vulnerable. When they are so concerned about another that whatever happens to them also happens to themselves, they extend the perimeters of their capacity to suffer—the happiness is shared, their injury is felt. When a loved person is devastated by death, the part of yourself you invested in another has been temporarily lost; the bereaved person is longing for the part given in love to another.

There is a perverse satisfaction in wallowing in the misery of loss and separation. Someone may misinterpret their feelings in such a way that they actually glorify their grief and try to hold on to it as a proof of their love and willingness to suffer. These negative responses cripple life and reduce it to partial existence, and are against the spirit of Islam.

When we recognise this loneliness and emptiness for what it is, we relieve to some extent the misgivings we may have about it. Whether we want to accept or believe it or not, our life does not end with the death of another, and likewise our capacity to love does not end with the loss of the object of our love. The capacity for love remains waiting for a chance to express itself a new in ways that can continue to enrich life. This is not disloyal.

One of the deepest needs of those in the distress of acute grief is to be kind to themselves, and it is not kind to entangle one's life and mind in a mass of fantasies and vehicles of self-deception. Nor is it useful to assume that one is so strong that one never needs help; for there are times in life when all of us can benefit from the strength, guidance, and wisdom of others.

Recovery from the wound of grief has been compared to recovery from a physical wound. Physicians can alleviate the pain and support the natural healing powers of physical wounds, but for the wound caused by the loss of a loved person every mourner needs special sympathy and support from the people around them.

Only when the lost person has been 'internalised' and become part of the bereaved, a part which can be integrated with their own personality and enrich it, is the mourning process complete, and adjustment to a new life can be made.

The final stage of mourning comes when the bereaved can calmly accept the loss of their loved ones, and turn to face renewed life without them. It is a time when they have often to acquire new skills—household management, cookery, driving a car, financial paperwork, etc. Although a painful time, it is also a time for personal growth possibilities and a new independence. It often brings a closer relationship with new other people.

The final farewell for a bereaved person comes when they can say goodbye to all their joint hopes, dreams and earthly plans and ambitions. Their thoughts and feelings have to slowly let go of dead one, for the wound left has to heal before that person can be whole again, with the dead person as a fond memory in the heart. It does not mean, of course, that the bereaved person has to say farewell to all memories of the loved one—as we have seen so clearly in the case of the Prophet ﷺ and his dear wife Khadijah.

This 'letting go' is a natural process which cannot be speeded up by anyone's help or by therapy. It may take a normal person from 9—12 months before they can begin to take their energy away from the deceased, and some 2-3 years before they are ready for new relationships. The Prophet ﷺ remained a widower for around a year before his aunt Khawlah urged him to consider his comfort and care, and the care of his four orphaned daughters, and take a new wife.

Many people live on without letting go of deceased for the rest of their lives; this may be acceptable, but they should be careful, and remember that if they have to face fresh losses, all the old grief will be opened up again.

Chapter 6

Special Types of Losses

There are certain modes and circumstances of death that require additional understanding—losses from suicide, sudden death, sudden infant death, miscarriage and stillbirth, abortion, and anticipated death. These can all create distinct problems for the bereaved, especially to Muslim families where suicide and abortion bring particular disgrace.

SUICIDE

Muslims believe that every soul and life has been created by God, and just as it is a great sin to kill any person unlawfully, so it is equally wrong to kill oneself. Islam views suicide so seriously because it is an affront to Allah, the Giver of Life. It is unacceptable for a Muslim to say to Allah, as it were, 'You gave me life, but I choose to take it away. 'Many Muslims view a person who has committed suicide as someone who has turned his or her back on Islam.

As it happens, Muslims do not accept that any person can 'cheat' God or die before their appointed time, no matter how they meet their death. To suggest otherwise is to suggest that some causes can over-rule

Allah's will, or negate His knowledge. The Islamic
belief is that if a person dies as the result of suicide, or
murder, accident or battle, they have nevertheless died
at the appointed time.

It is obvious that people do die from all these
causes, but whereas one may say that God knew that
if certain circumstances pertained then this or that
person would die in this or that manner, it is not correct
to assume that God caused their death from suicide, or
murder, or accident, or warfare. Allah does not wish
any person to take his or her own life.

> 'Allah wants to lighten your difficulties, for
> humans were created weak....do not kill your-
> selves; truly Allah has been merciful to you.'
> (4:28-29).

> 'How can you reject faith in Allah, seeing you
> were without life and He gave you life; and
> He will cause you to die, and will bring you
> again to life.' (2:28).

People who commit suicide are in a terrible state
of stress; they have lost *sabr* (faithful patience). Life no
longer seems worth living. However, Islam teaches
that it is not realistic to believe that any human being
should expect to pass his or her entire lifetime without
hardships and sufferings. On the contrary, we are told
to expect them, and be ready for them, so that when
they strike they can be faced up to with courage and
fortitude. The trials and tribulations of earthly life are
not pointless, but should be consciously regarded as a
test for Afterlife. Moreover, no person has knowledge

of what new events, opportunities and joys will come to the stressed person later in life. We may be in despair, but we do not know what work Allah still wants us to do, or what earthly reward He may yet bestow after our patient suffering. Not even the very worst of calamities should make a Muslim consider suicide out of despair, if their faith in God is genuine.

Anas recorded: 'None of you should wish for death for any calamity that befalls you, but should say: 'O Allah! Cause me to live so long as my life is better for me, and cause me to die when death is better for me.' (Abu Dawud 3102, Muslim 6480).

Many righteous but rather insensitive people express the view that all suicides have died as unbelievers, not in a state of faith, because they have forgotten to be aware of God's mercy and have disobeyed Him; the unfortunate result will be their inevitable punishment in Hell. This, however, is only a very partial picture. It does not take account of God's mercy, or allow room for interpretation of what exactly the Prophet ﷺ meant in his few hadiths on the subject.

Thabit ibn al-Dhhak recorded that the Blessed Messenger ﷺ observed: He who killed himself with steel, or poison, or threw himself off a mountain would be tormented on the Day of Resurrection with that very thing.' (See Muslim 199-208).

It is obvious that the soul of the suicide will indeed be grievously tormented by the full awareness of knowing what he or she has done to the loved ones left behind; this is not the same thing as being consigned to a place of punishment for wicked people and nonbelievers.

Those bereaved by a suicide should try to remember that if it is true that there is life after death, then any person attempting to escape from their stress and problems by taking their own life will not succeed—because they continue to exist. Not only that, but in expanded consciousness they may now experience even more stress, for they may be allowed to see the terrible aftermath of their desperate action, the agonies of hurt and despair they have caused. It is worth pointing this out to depressed people threatening to commit suicide, to make them stop and think.

When the Blessed Prophet ﷺ commented that people who killed themselves would be tormented by what they had done in the Afterlife, it was very true. The suicide no doubt bitterly regrets doing it, but there is no way they can stop the hurt they have caused; they cannot go back and they have to come to terms with that awful awareness.

Incidentally, Allah made it clear in the Qur'an that even if individuals who had died got the oportunity to come back to warn and enlighten those on this side of life, it would be to no avail. People determined not to believe would not be shifted in their determination, even if someone came to them from the dead. They would think up some other comfortable explanation for their 'hallucination.'

> 'Even if we sent angels to them, and the dead
> spoke to them, and we gathered together all

things before their very eyes, they are not the
ones to believe, unless it is in God's plan. Most
of them ignore the truth.' (6:111).

Obviously, if a Muslim has real faith in Allah and
life after death, suicide can never be thought of as an
escape, and this is one reason why education regarding death-bed experiences and the Qur'anic teachings
and hadiths about life after death are so important in
a practical sense. Another aspect of the punishment of
the soul of the suicide is that all individuals are called
to account for the hurts and damage they cause others.
Obviously, when a person commits suicide, they *do*
hurt and damage others, sometimes affecting those
who mourn for them for the rest of their lives. More is
said about this later.

The Prophet ﷺ himself used prayers to help
overcome the causes of depression, and advised para-
phrasing his words according to the situation in which
people found themselves. For example: 'My Lord, I
seek refuge with you against worry and depression,
disability and laziness, cowardliness and miserliness,
being overburdened with debt and being subject to
oppression'—most of the things that drive unfortu-
nates to consider suicide today!

Depression is always much more easily dispelled
when a Muslim remembers that everything in life is in
the 'hands' of Allah. They are able to look at life with
its sufferings and misfortunes in a more detached and
reasonable way.

The minds of people who commit or attempt

suicide are always zoned in upon their own painful situation. The two most common thoughts uppermost are either 'How can I stop, or get out of this painful situation?' or 'All this is your fault, and you'll be sorry now that I've killed myself!' Frequently, of course, the suicide did not really intend to end their life at all, and hoped to be saved at the last moment; they were really only intending to 'punish' their loved ones, by making a dramatic gesture as a cry for help.

Either way, they are feeling so desperate that it is a very sad situation. If a believer actually follows through and deliberately commits suicide it can be regarded as a sinful act because it is defiance of the will of God, and it is extremely unpleasant for those left behind and a deliberate cruelty to them.

For the bereaved, there is not only the sense of loss, but also a legacy of shame, fear, rejection, anger and guilt. The suicide has sentenced the survivors to deal with the horror of the persistent thought that it was all their fault—they may have not tried hard enough, or they may have said or done something to trigger it off. They feel they may have either caused the suicide, or at least, failed to stop it.

Suicide is the most difficult bereavement crisis for any family to face. Firstly, there is the feeling of shame. Not only has the suicide 'failed' in life, but the family has also 'failed' and let the suicide down, by being unable to prevent them, cure them or give them hope. This shame can drastically affect the interactions of the bereaved with each other and with society.

The same is true whether the suicide is successful, or only attempted.

The second major emotion is guilt—the bereaved often take responsibility for the action of the suicide and have a strong feeling that there must have been something they should or could have done to prevent the death. This guilt feeling is particularly powerful when there actually was some conflict between the deceased and the bereaved.

Sometimes the guilt is felt so strongly that the bereaved do not ever really recover from the loss, but punish themselves in various ways, or begin to act in such a way that society punishes them—adults break down or become recluses, or turn to drugs and alcohol. Children frequently become delinquent.

The bereaved also feel intense anger. Not only are they angry about the waste of the life of the loved one, with all its potential and unknown future, but perhaps they are also angry because a great deal of their effort *had* gone into trying to help that person, all to no avail. They might also perceive the death as a personal rejection—'Why did he do this to me?' This rage then goes on to fuel their guilt feelings, because of its intensity. It is not uncommon to hear the bereaved state that if the deceased had not killed himself/herself they felt like killing them themselves, for what they were putting them through.

Along with the anger comes low self-esteem; the bereaved parent, spouse or fiance cannot help feeling that they were not good enough; they have been rejected. They assume that the suicide could not have thought enough of them, that their help and support must have been inadequate, or that the suicide might even have been trying to escape from them and could see no other way of doing it. This traumatic sense of failure can even lead to self-destructive impulses in the bereaved; if they cannot throw off this trauma they spend their future lives carrying a sense of doom. It is an awful truth that suicide can sometimes 'run in families', the bereaved in one instance becoming potential suicides themselves later.

Apart from the 'usual' bereavement therapy, in these cases the bereaved need 'curing' of any distorted thinking, and they need consoling with particularly generous sympathy. The urge to commit suicide generally builds up over a long period, perhaps with numerous scenes, threats, bluff-calling and failed attempts. The suicide's family has probably been coping with a great deal of stress and depression for some time, usually calling on reserves of love and patience way over and above the normal call of duty.

It is vital that the bereaved person accepts that the fact that the suicide was not ultimately prevented is *not the fault or responsibility of the grieved family*. Every person goes through traumas and challenges in life and normally they manage to survive without contemplating suicide. People who have come through suffering to a more tranquil existence later are frequently angry, frustrated and aggrieved and do not sympathise with the attitude of the one who has 'packed it all in,' and given up.

Sometimes, they try to find a way out of their guilt by seeing the victim's behaviour not as a suicide but as an accidental death, and a myth is created that disguises what really happened, thus avoiding the necessary stage of facing up to reality. It is extremely difficult for Muslims to talk about what really happened in suicide cases to other Muslims, partly because some zealots will encourage them to regard all suicides as sinners to be 'cast off' from the mind and consigned to Hell—a grief therapist can prove very helpful in these circumstances.

Much of the guilt is unrealistic, and making the bereaved face up to reality can bring enormous relief. Sometimes, of course, the guilt is real because the bereaved *were* in some way responsible for the suicide's feelings of failure, and in these cases they need help to deal with these feelings if they are not to punish themselves consciously or subconsciously for the rest of their lives. They have to be allowed to see that everyone makes mistakes, has rows, says things they do not really mean, and that God really does forgive, so long as they honestly face up to their faults and are genuinely sorry. It can bring great relief to the bereaved to pray for the soul of the suicide, and believe in their hearts that the suicide will appreciate their thoughts, and that they can forgive each other.

It is incorrect to insist that all suicides cannot be forgiven. Allah made it crystal clear that there was only one sin that could not be forgiven—the sin of dying in the state of shirk.

> 'God forgives not (the sin of) joining other Gods with Him; but He forgives whom He pleases all other sins than this.' (4:116).

> 'O My servants, who have transgressed against their own souls! Despair not of the mercy of God; for God forgives all sins; He is Oft-Forgiving, Most Merciful.' (39:53).

> 'Not for you is the decision whether He turn in mercy to them, or punish them; for they are indeed wrongdoers. To God belongs everything that is in the heavens and on earth; He forgives who He pleases, and punishes who He pleases; but God is Oft-Forgiving, Most Merciful.' (3:128-129).

There is at least one record of a man committing suicide at the time of the Prophet ﷺ. The Prophet ﷺ did not offer the janazah prayer for him, but he did tell his companions to offer it. When they did, they obviously prayed Allah to forgive him. Therefore, it seems quite permissible to pray for others who have committed suicide.

This is great consolation, for it means that if God wills—the suicide can be prayed for without feeling guilty, and may indeed have already found the peace from stressed so desired in life.

Having thought these comforting thoughts, next the bereaved Muslims have to be encouraged to have faith in God by accepting the comfort that if Allah can forgive them, then they should put the burden down, and forgive themselves.

It is common for the bereaved to fantasise about the characters of suicides, either regarding them as having been all good nor all bad—neither of which is reality. Those who create an idealised character for the deceased (and consequently suffer all the more deep guilt for their death) have to be made to see that this is not reality; in fact, their 'ideal loved one' was probably a considerable trial and worry to others, and was quite likely suffering from deep clinical depression, saw no way out, and in desperation took his or her own life. Once the bereaved can realise that the suicide was the victim of a clinical state which was not in any way their fault, they can relieve themselves of the heavy burden of guilt.

It is also helpful to realise that shame, guilt, anger and fear are all quite normal stages to go through—the bereaved can observe where they are in the process, and note their own progress towards recovery.

The chief consolation to offer Muslims is to widen their consciousness of God's mercy and compassion. Not every person who commits suicide is a wilful kafir; *clinical depression is just as much a 'disease' as any other illness, and people suffering from it are victims, not wilfully evil people.*

Probably the most important hadith to bear in mind in this situation is one recorded by Aishah:

'There are three (categories of people) whose actions are not recorded (against them); a sleeper (who is unconscious) until he wakes, a (person with) dis-

turbed mind until he or she is restored to reason, and
a child below the age of puberty.' (Abu Dawud 4384).

The meaning is crystal clear: Allah does not hold
against individuals any sins or mistakes committed
when they were not responsible for their actions or
when the balance of their mind was disturbed. In fact,
Shariat law concurs that if any people in these categories commit any crimes they should not be punished,
and if they make agreements or enter into contracts
under these conditions, they should not be considered
valid. Since the vast majority of suicides obviously fall
into this category, this should be a major consolation to
those Muslims struggling with their grief for such a
person.

No matter what human beings conclude, it is to be
stressed that Allah alone knows the truth of every
circumstance, and fortunately for us, His mercy is so
much greater than ours. It is too simplistic to assume
that the suicide has just given up faith in God and has
died a non-believer. Sometimes the suicide's 'cry for
help' is just as much a cry to God for help as it is a cry
to other human beings, and therefore—although their
act is wrong and based on a wrong understanding of
Allah's will for them—it can nevertheless be regarded
as a cry from the position of that person's faith and
belief, and not out of their unbelief. And every Muslim
who dies in faith will not lose his or her reward.

Remember this beautiful promise given by Allah
to the Prophet 鷺, and remember it well, and cherish it:

'If a person has in the heart the goodness to the

weight of one barely corn, and has said, There is no God but Me, they shall come out of Hell-fire.' (Hadith Qudsi, Ezzedine Ibrahim, Beirut, 1980).

SUDDEN DEATH

This includes accidental death, heart attacks and homicides. Once again, these circumstances are more difficult to grieve than deaths where there has been prior warning.

Sudden deaths leave the survivors with a sense of unreality about the loss which may last a long time. It is so hard to believe that a person who 'died in good health' is really not there any more, and there is a great sense of 'unfinished business.' It is not unusual for the bereaved to feel completely numb and walk round in a daze, not really facing up to the loss for a long time. Crying and grief may be long delayed.

When it comes, the kind of guilt expressed is usually that of the self-blame and 'if only' type—'if only I had been with him', 'if only I had not let him do that,' 'if only he had regular check-ups.'

> 'Don't be like the unbelievers who say of their brethren, when they are travelling through the earth or engaged in fighting: 'If only they had stayed with us, they would not have died or been slain.' (3:156).

The bereaved have to face up to reality about this, and also to the fact that any reaction of strong anger they might have is quite normal. There is a natural need in these cases to blame someone—inadequacies of the medical service, carelessness of other road users, friends who had led the deceased astray, and so on. In some sudden deaths there may have to be inquest or even a trial, which adds to the problem if the judicial procedure is slow. Until the whole process is finalised, the bereaved are unable to let the deceased go, and so the grieving process can be long delayed. On the other hand, this is not always a bad thing. It can sometimes help the bereaved to arrive at the acceptance of loss when it all comes to its final conclusion.

Other features in cases of sudden death are the feeling of helplessness and frustration, and frequently rage against the hospital staff or drivers of friends involved at the death. The stress of sudden death seems to trigger off the 'fight or flight' responses, and leads to agitated depression. Quite often God gets the blame—for not saving the person; the bereaved then also have to cope with their feelings of rejection of and hatred for God as well as the loss of the loved one. This is a particular tussle for Muslims, who know that it is their duty to accept with patience and not turn against Allah.

The bereaved also have regrets for unfinished business, things they did not have the chance to say or do concerning the deceased. It is worth considering that the deceased might also be suffering from considerable frustration, too. I can remember once being busily involved in some matter and on my way home on my motorbike when a parked driver suddenly threw open his car door and missed me by a whisker.

I would have been furious to have died like that, without any warning, in the best of health, with things to do that I was deeply involved in doing; even accepting that God must have intended that to be my time, it would still have come as a shock, and I might not have been as composed and resigned to it as I ought to have been. I might have been in the middle of an argument; I might have said and done things that needed someone's forgiveness; I might not have told someone important that I loved them. Can you imagine my regrets at being snatched away without the chance to put things right? So, perhaps the best way to help the bereaved left behind in those cases is to try to find some way of closure for any 'unfinished business'.

It is not really any consolation to say things like 'at least you've still got your husband/wife/children', or 'everything's going to be all right'. It is helpful, however, to let the bereaved come to acknowledge that the deceased really was loved and really is dead, and then to help them to see that they are not the only ones who have suffered these circumstances—they will be able to go on, and others, hopefully, will help them.

Muslims should try to strengthen the faith of the bereaved, and bring them to accept the reality of the inevitable laws of nature which do not spare an individual, no matter how much loved, from being hit by the car, drowned by the flood, crushed by the falling wall, shot by the bullet, or struck down by disease. Allah knows every circumstance, and the most helpful thing is to allow the bereaved to feel loved by God, and that the deceased was and is also loved by God, even in these tragic circumstances.

> 'If you are killed, or die in the way of God, forgiveness and mercy from God are far better than all they could amass. And if you die or are killed, lo! It is to God that you are brought together.' (3:157-158).

SUDDEN INFANT DEATH—(COT DEATH)

This occurs in infants under one year of age, usually between two and six months. The causes are not fully known, but probably include accident and viral infections. Parents often conclude that their baby suffocated, choked, or had some previously unsuspected illness.

As the death occurs without warning, the parents are not prepared for the loss; and as there is absence of definite cause, there is considerable guilt and blame. Any mother, who has barely recovered from all the tiredness and upheaval of pregnancy and childbirth, and whose consciousness is naturally almost competely wrapped up in the new baby, would be totally shattered and distraught.

It is only natural for everyone to wonder why the baby died, which inevitably casts the suspicion that somehow the parents really were to blame, perhaps through their carelessness, ignorance or neglect.

As with other sudden death, there is a need for investigation, and often the police are involved. In these days of increasing child abuse and neglect, quite innocent parents are often put through the ordeal of being questioned and even held in custody—which inevitably adds to the stress.

A major factor to be considered in infant death which often goes overlooked is the effect on other children in the family. Parents should be very alert to this, for these brothers and sisters often suffer enormous guilt. They may have previously been jealous of the new arrival, and wished they had not been born, or that they could get rid of them. Some of them even believe that it was their nasty thoughts that killed them, as if by magic.

The biggest cause of guilt for the parents is the 'if only' syndrome—'if only I had been awake at that time,' 'if only I had checked once more,' 'if only I had not laid him on his face.' They need help to realise that they must forgive themselves—it is quite unrealistic for any parent to be awake and watching twenty-four hours per day. They have not neglected the infant, their sleep is not to blame for the infant's death.

Sadly, because of lack of communication and guidance, there is often disharmony in the marriage afterwards when an infant dies; wives may feel that their husbands do not care enough about the death if they keep a 'stiff upper lip' and do not always cry when they do. Yet the poor husband may be doing his best to cope with his own grief and a despairing wife by trying to calm things down and normalise the situation. He will sooner or later resent being accused of lack of concern or understanding. Inevitably mothers feel deep distress because they feel so close to a child that has issued from their own body; a father should not be blamed if he cannot share the same 'maternal instincts'.

Some women may fear renewed sexual relations in case there is another pregnancy and the experience is repeated. They frequently suffer pressure from people who encourage them to rush into another pregnancy as soon as possible to make up for the loss. (This may not be a bad idea, but pressurising people only adds to their stress).

Many women are appalled by the attitude of some well-meaning people, especially men, that a baby is easily replaced, and one can have another one next year to make up for it. Some people seem to have no realisation whatsoever of how quickly tiny little people become much loved individuals. To suggest that a baby is just a little object and one is much like another seems to be completely callous and lacking in understanding as regards the intimate and deeply loving relationship between mother and child throughout pregnancy, childbirth and the short life of the precious dead infant. If bereaved women can accept that this attitude is not intended unkindly, but only stems from their ignorance of the experience of maternal feelings, it may help to tone down their resentment towards them.

Sometimes, when a baby dies in hospital, the parents can be refused permission to be with the little deceased one, to hold it and love it in farewell. Hospitals should be encouraged to be more humane about this, and allow the parents time to come to terms with the death, and grieve with the little body if they wish.[1]

Sometimes the baby has to have an autopsy, and this can be very traumatic. The staff responsible for the autopsy can help a great deal if they can reassure the parents about the cause of the death—it is much easier to accept if they know it was nobody's fault but was inevitable.

Once again, Muslims have to try to exercise their patience; as we have seen so often, it is not given to us always to know the will of God, but we have to accept it. Parents should be allowed full opportunity to grieve the loss of the little one, and to be assured that their innocent souls are safe with Him.

The Prophet ﷺ always insisted that children who died before their parents went as forerunners for their parents in the life Hereafter, and would serve as 'protection' against Hell-fire. (Muslim 6365-6368, 6371-6372).

There is also one very interesting hadith that mentions the continued loving existence of little ones that die, that could act as great consolation to parents in this sad case, for it suggests that even after physical and earthly death the soul of the child does not forsake its earthly parents, but remains very close to them until

---

1. In the case of Muslim infants, there are certain guidelines laid down. See p. 75.

they are rejoined in Paradise.

Abu Hassan recorded: I told Abu Hurayrah that my two children had died. Would he relate to me anything from Allah's Messenger ﷺ a hadith that would soothe our hearts in our bereavement? He said: 'Yes. Small children are the birds of Paradise. If one of them meets his parents he would take hold of his clothing, (or he said, with his hand) as I take hold of the hem of your clothing (with my hand). And he (the child) would not take (his hand) off it until Allah causes his parent to enter Paradise.' (Muslim 6370).

It is a lovely and consoling image—the child never severing its link with the parent, and following their progress throughout their lives until, Insha'Allah, they are re-united.

These hadiths should, of course, be understood within the general framework of the fundamental principles of Islam. For example, it is no use a sinful person being confident of forgiveness because one (or some) of his or her children have died. No matter how many children a person loses in their infancy, they will not be able to earn reprieve for the parent at the time of judgement. Similarly, if a parent has killed a child, the two will stand in front of Allah to judge between them, for Allah does not allow the rights of any of His servants to go unaccounted for, and that includes the youngest of them. (See 81: 7-9, 11, 14 on p. 73). The children themselves will not be accountable, since they have died before they reach the age of accountability.

MISCARRIAGE, STILLBIRTHS AND ABORTIONS

Miscarriages are defined here as the death of a baby during the pregnancy despite medical efforts to save it, and stillbirth as a full or near full-term baby being born dead. The term abortion is used here to denote pregnancies that have been terminated deliberately, at the wish of the mother or any other agent.

Usually, when a woman loses a baby before time (forty weeks), everyone's first concern is for the mother's health, and the miscarried or stillborn or aborted foetus is swiftly removed from sight and consciousness, and disposed of as if it had not been a proper living being and potential person with a soul or his or her own. The pregnant mother with the child moving within her, is usually highly conscious of her unborn infant as a real person, but frequently the general public does not really regard them as separate individuals until they are actually born. It is also the case that many women do not develop awareness of their *first* baby as a real person until the baby is born, despite all the education and pictures available. Somehow, to these girls, it just doesn't seen real until the baby is there in front of them. When an infant is born dead, especially in the first half of pregnancy, some carers focus only on whether or not the woman will be able to bear future children, and ignore completely her sense of loss and the loss of the potential new human being. Calling the unborn child a foetus is also not helpful in these circumstances. It may be the correct technical term for the baby at various stages of development before birth, but it is a term that de-personalises that tiny living person. Needless to say, this de-personalisation is done quite deliberately by those who wish to promote the freedom of abortion on demand, or who feel this is the best way to de-sensitise the maternal feelings of the mother who has lost the baby. Many grieving mothers feel affronted and offended by this, and it is hurtful to them.

Anyone who has gone through loss of an unborn child knows very well that this loss can be severe, even if others try to 'sweep it under the carpet,' minimise it in their attempts to cheer up the bereft mothers, or even hide the event if it has embarrassed their family. If the miscarriage occurs very early, it generally does not affect the mother too much, because she regards it as little more than a disappointment to her wish for pregnancy; she has usually not got to the stage where the foetus is recognisable to her as a child. A very early miscarriage therefore seems to be not much more than just a heavy period.

However, once the mother has seen that the child within her has shaped up as a child, it is a very different matter. In previous generations, mothers generally became conscious of the actual existence of another being within their body about the 16th week. This is when the movements made by the unborn child are usually first felt by the mother. This was called 'the quickening', and many believed that it was at this stage that the soul (if there was one) entered the child's body, and it became a separate person. Following this logic, if the death of the foetus occurred before this time it was not as serious as if it occurred after the quickening.

Modern technical knowledge has changed this view drastically. It is now possible to see the unborn moving and developing baby from the earliest of times. As ultra-sound equipment continues to improve, these sights will become much more familiar. It has already made it possible to actually film the controlled death of an unborn baby when abortion takes place. Opinions are very divided on the wisdom of showing this—some regard it as part of everyday general knowledge, perhaps suitable material for personal and social education classes, whereas others regard it as horrendously gruesome and able to cause permanent trauma. Others regard this as the vital shock-tactics needed to make people face reality, and thus protect the unborn, and prevent casual abortions.

The hadith quoted in the previous section can be a great consolation to these mothers too; they are assured that the little one has not ceased to exist, but his or her soul is safe in the hands of Allah. It is enormous comfort to a bereaved mother of a deceased little baby to be assured that those who die young escape accountability, and are directly ushered into Jannah. Moreover, it is said that on the Day of the Judgement, such little ones will hold the fingers of their parents and will take them to Paradise.

Mothers of stillborn babies experience a lot of self-blame; they torture themselves, trying to work out if they had unwittingly been responsible for damaging their baby. Was it caused by their taking unwise or violent exercise, such as horse-riding or motor-bike riding? Was it due to eating the wrong things, not eating enough, over-eating, or smoking? Was the baby damaged because of her husband's sexual activities? Husbands are frequently the target for the wife's anger—and if they are trying to be strong and supportive after the tragedy a wife may misinterpret this as 'not caring'.

Mothers often blame fathers for not having the same feelings, as we suggested in the previous section concerning infant-death. Many husbands get their back-up help from a doctor who is also a man, and who may share the same point of view as the husband. They do not want to see the wife in the agony of anguish. They want to calm things down and restore normality as quickly as possible. This is usually out of kindness and concern, and not because they are callous and don't care. However, it is worth repeating that it may be well meant, but it generally does not help a woman who has lost a child to be told that it doesn't matter, she should try again, and have another child as quickly as possible (rather like climbing back on the horse or bike as soon as possible after falling off). This might be good advice, but it strikes many women as highly insensitive, and not at all what they want to hear at this time. It virtually denies the existence and importance of the baby for whom the mother is grieving. All mothers should be allowed their time to grieve. Seeing the dead foetus often helps to focus on the reality of the loss, but hospitals do not always allow this, or only do it reluctantly. If a foetus has been surgically removed, moreover, it will very likely be in a very upsetting condition and cut into pieces. When this is the case, if the mother is demanding to see her baby's remains, her husband should perhaps be told the truth so that he may persuade her otherwise.

The 1996 medical document 'Foetal sentience' is just one presentation of the evidence that unborn babies have all the anatomical structures present and functioning by the 6th-7th week. Dr. Abdul Majid Katue, the Muslim co-ordinator for the Society for the Protection of Unborn Children, welcomed the report (Muslim News, 27 Sept., 1996) and pointed out how it proved scientifically, at the end of the C20, what the Prophet had said in the C7: 'When forty-two nights (6 weeks) have passed over that which is conceived, Allah sends an angel who shapes it, makes it ears, eyes, skin, flesh and bones. Then he says : O Lord, is it male or female? And your Lord decides what He wishes, and then the angel records it.

This author has seen with her own eyes on the ultra-sound screen that a little boy really is identifiable as a boy at 6 weeks, and has watched the traumatic process of the destruction and removal of a foetus in typical hospital procedure. Once having seen, it becomes very difficult to regard any death of unborn infants in a casual manner.

This is not the place, however, to argue the rights and wrongs of abortion, but to consider how to console the bereaved parents.

Bereaved parents frequently find that people are uncomfortable about talking to them about their loss, and this does not help them resolve their grief. Sometimes family and friends are actually critical of their grief, and feel they are making a fuss about nothing.

It is important to realise that they have sustained a real death, and the loss should not be minimised.

Cases of abortion are highly sensitive, because inevitably the mother really is to blame for the death of her child, and the guilt is very real. Some get their guilt much delayed. As previously commented, many women who have not actually given birth to a full-term baby do not have fully-developed awareness of the reality of the child, and push aside any feelings of guilt others try to engender in them. They may try to completely suppress and forget any incipient feelings. However, it is a fact that in almost every case, the guilt and grief *will* surface later on—perhaps when the woman has more knowledge—and she will have to face the torment of wondering what the child she destroyed might have been.

She may be quite unable to forgive herself; she may feel God will never forgive her. Allah expressed quite clearly that abortion is unacceptable to Him, and therefore it should not really be contemplated by a Muslim.

The following verses talk about children that have

been born alive, but the principle extends back to the unborn. 'Do not slay your children because of poverty—We will provide for you and for them.' (6:151).

> 'Slay not your children...the killing of them is a great sin. Do not take life, which Allah has made sacred, except for just cause.' (17:31-33; 5:68).

> 'When the souls are sorted out; when the female infant buried alive, (the Arabian method of birth control before the time of the Prophet) is asked for what crime she was killed;...when the World on High is unveiled...then shall each soul know what it has put forward.' (81:7-9, 11,14).

The only grounds Muslims should contemplate for abortion are if the mother's life has genuinely been placed in danger by the pregnancy. In that case, Islamic law takes the view that the actual life of the existing mother takes precedence over the potential life of the unborn child. Mere social inconvenience is not acceptable grounds for abortion.

Controversy rages in the western world over the rights of a woman to abort her unborn child, with most religious people feeling that the unborn child is being denied the right to live. Islam takes the point of view that once God has given life and a soul to a human body nobody has the right to take that life, and therefore abortion is wrong. It is very important, when counselling a pregnant girl, to point out that many women who have abortions often regard it as a solution to their problems at that time, only to discover enormous problems of depression, guilt, and possible inability to have other children later.

Many women in these circumstances try to convince themselves that the foetuses are not real 'beings', but just 'part of their bodies'. This is not logical, and guilt feelings based on the reality of the unborn child will always surface later. Many women who have abortions are ashamed and in a state of panic, and once it is over often feel that the best way to deal with it is to put it out of their minds as quickly as possible—but by doing this, once again they rob themselves of the grieving process, and it will surface later.

The surface experience of many mothers who end a pregnancy they had not wished for is usually one of relief initially but a woman who does not mourn the loss may well experience great unresolved grief.

Sometimes the mother involved is only a young girl, and her parents are very angry with her; sometimes they also get angry not only because she got pregnant in the first place, but also because she then killed the baby, which, after all, would have been their grandchild. Grandparents should not be overlooked by those helping the bereaved.

However, censure and abuse of women and girls who have had abortions is unbecoming from those who are not in a position to know all the circumstances involved, as Allah is. Medical practitioners in most societies will terminate pregnancies for various reasons, interpreting the 'threat to life or sanity' of the mother involved quite widely. What they do not generally approve is the notion of abortion on demand, for casual social reasons.

Anyone who has seen tiny premature babies struggling for life in the same hospital where others of similar age and size are terminated, will tell you it is *not* a casual matter. Moreover, the women who have abortions usually do not do it casually at all, but suffer great anguish and distress and pain. So, people involved with cases of abortion should remember that very important hadith that those whose balance of mind is disturbed are not held responsible by Allah. They should take some consolation from that, if that was indeed the case.

In true Islam, no child should be born outside of marriage, and this is the ideal to be aimed at. In some societies, the harsh solution to the problem is to put the unwed mother to death. To be realistic in a western society, the best solution is to encourage a pregnant girl to have the baby and not abort it, and then see to it that the innocent child and the foolish mother are both properly cared for.

Even better is to solve the problem of 'unwanted' pregnancies by encouraging menfolk to be honourable, responsible, kind and considerate in their sexual activity, and to make sure that their women-folk are adequately protected each time they have intercourse when a pregnancy is not desired.

NEO-NATAL DEATH AND BURIAL

In most schools of Islamic thought, babies born after four months of gestation (16 weeks) should be washed and buried with a funeral prayer performed for them, whereas if they have died before the 16th week, they just need to be buried. Some scholars have said that babies should only receive the funeral prayer if they showed signs of life before dying—for example, crying, sneezing, movement. However, most schools agree that this should not be insisted upon.

Al-Mughirah ibn Shubah recorded: 'A (mourner who is) riding should go behind the bier, and those on foot should walk behind it, in front of it, on its right and on its left, keeping near it. Prayer should be offered over an abortion, and forgiveness and mercy supplicated for its parents.' (Abu Dawud 3174).

Ibn Umar, Ibn Sirin and Ibn al-Musayyab maintain that prayer should be said over every aborted baby, whether it has drawn breath and cried or not. Ahmad ibn Hanbal and Ishaq ibn Rahwaih hold that funeral prayers are not required for an aborted foetus less than four months and ten days old, on the principle that they believed it was at this stage that the individual living soul enters the unborn child (when the infant in the womb 'quickens'). After the quickening, prayers should be said, for the unborn child is an individual. However, as we have pointed out earlier, these authorities did not have the knowledge presented by modern equipment. Ibn Abbas, Jabir and Abu Hanifah take the point of view that if the child draws breath and cries after birth, then prayer should be said for it, but not if it dies without 'giving voice'. That is also the view of Malik, al-Auzal and al-Shafi'i. (Awn al-Mabud, III, p 179).

In many hospitals aborted foetuses are routinely taken and incinerated, without the parents even seeing their dead child. Some unenlightened hospitals even take the point of view that it is wrong and morbid for a parent to want to see a dead foetus, and treat the bereaved parent with disgust and amazement if they ask to do so. Muslims should be aware of this, and request that Muslim babies are not dealt with in the ordinary routine way of hospital disposal of dead foetuses.

It is the most desired practice for all hospitals, doctors and midwives to have telephone numbers of local mosques and Imams, so that they may advise them promptly of the deaths of premature or neo-natal babies in hospital, and to be sensitive to the difference between the Islamic ritual washing and the simple cleansing that nurses might give a dead child. If possible, the parents and relatives should be allowed privacy to carry out the washing ceremony and the shrouding. Hospitals should then allow the parents to take the baby out of the hospital for burial—some are happy to allow this, others take a strongly disapproving attitude, perhaps fearing that the little corpses will not be disposed of properly (although there is nothing proper about mass incineration!).

Muslim babies should not be cremated or incinerated. However, whether taken by parents and buried
properly, or cremated in the hospital, the funeral
prayers for the little one can be recited at any time,
before burial or after.

More than one ceremony of funeral prayer is
possible for people who missed the first session. Prayers
can be said at the graveyard, but it is just as suitable,
if not preferable, if they are done elsewhere—for
example in the mosque or in the home. Prayers can be
performed abroad for a deceased child, either in a
group with an Imam or without, it does not matter.

All the family can participate in funeral prayers,
providing they are in a position to do so. Distraught
bereaved mothers should try not to scream and wail,
but remember that all souls are in the hand of God, and
that He is the Bestower of Life and also the One Who
takes it away, and that any soul received into His hands
is in the care of the Most Compassionate and Benefi-
cent One.

ANTICIPATED GRIEF

Anticipated grief is when grieving is started prior
to an actual death because the death involved is taking
a very long time as a person gradually succumbs to
fatal illness, or is kept in forlorn hope on a life support
machine. This is different from 'survivor grief'. If there
is a long period of anticipation, the potential survivor
begins the process of grieving well in advance, and

particular problems may arise. The most common is inner guilt at the resentment of the 'burden' caused by the unfortunate dying person. If they are difficult to cope with or nurse, and go on and on living past the expected time instead of dying when expected, carers may begin to 'run out of steam'; it is not that they lack sympathy, but it seems to reach a limit when they are no longer really sharing feelings with the sick or aged one, and then—when the death eventually does occur, they may be struck by appalling guilt and shame at their 'callousness'. They feel that all their efforts are set at naught, because they have lacked sympathy for a helpless dying person that they ought to have been loving.

Sometimes the awareness of the inevitability of death alternates with the denial that the event is going to happen. There are a whole variety of feelings involved—an increase of anxiety, a withdrawal and freeing of emotional ties from the loved deceased. There is also a strong personal death awareness—as you watch someone else deteriorate during a progressive illness you cannot help but identify with the process yourself, and become acutely aware that this may one day be your own fate too. When people watch their parents die, they have the strong feeling that now they have moved up a generation, and are one step nearer their own turn.

People who are obliged to anticipate someone's death frequently (and quite sensibly) practise 'role rehearsal' for what will happen after the death has

taken place—'What will I do with the children?',
'Where will I live?' 'How will I manage?' This is quite
normal and should not be thought wrong, but it is
often disapproved of by those who regard it as tactless,
unkind and socially unacceptable behaviour to regard
a dying person as if they were already dead. A person
who talks about what they will do after the death is
seen as insensitive, premature, and their comments in
bad taste. Yet the worries are very real, and it is foolish
not to make sensible plans.

The worst thing that can happen from the dying
person's point of view is that the griever can withdraw
emotionally from them far too soon, long before they
have died. Sometimes relatives start to make plans for
what they will do when they die, for example holidays
and visits they will make, only to discover that the
person unobligingly does not pass away according to
plan but lives on and on; they feel trapped, and even
resentful, if they feel they cannot make any arrangements for themselves until the person dies. This inevitably hurts the feelings of the dying one, and leads to
guilt for the resentment in the bereaved once the
person has died.

Sometimes the opposite can happen, and the family can move too close to the dying one, trying to
overmanage the patient's care. Some go to the most
extreme means to keep a person alive, seeking all sorts
of treatments, encouraging them to undergo one desperate operation after another, which can actually be
quite distressing for some patients. Most people fear

and dislike operations; when people know that they are dying, they might much prefer to remain in control of what is done or not done to their poor suffering bodies. Sometimes they would much rather not die stuffed with tubes and stuck with needles, put through one unpleasant treatment after another. They would rather let nature take its course, and return their souls to God when He sees fit.

When there is a long wait for death, the best use of this time is in care of unfinished business—both in practical matters, and also in saying things that need saying. It is of enormous help if, instead of concentrating on impending tragedy, the persons involved can regard this as an opportunity to take care of things that need dealing with, and a chance to put disaffection right.

Don't forget that the dying one is also condemned to suffer from this anticipatory grief—the dying person is going to 'lose' everyone, and the anticipation of loss can sometimes be overwhelming. Sometimes they 'turn their faces to the wall' in order to cope with these feelings.

EUTHANASIA AND TERRIBLE SUFFERING

Sometimes carers are brought face to face with the question of euthanasia. This is a Greek word implying a 'good death', and what it generally means is that if a loved one is suffering in an appalling condition, or has been damaged beyond all hope of recovery in an accident, or is on some sort of life-support machinery, should their lives be ended by son eone else, who means well? Should the medics go on and on trying everything to save that person, or should they cease their efforts and allow the patient to die peacefully, painlessly, and with as much dignity as possible?

You often hear people state that they would not leave animals to suffer in dreadful pain, so it ought to be permissible, in some circumstances, to put a deliberate end to a human being's life.

For Muslims, this is forbidden. The termination of human life belongs to Allah. When people interfere with this, they are actually guilty of killing. Euthanasia is defined as 'mercy killing', which clearly acknowledges that it is killing, and all killing is forbidden in Islam except as punishment for certain well defined crimes. Even if a person makes clear that he or she wishes to die, and even if this wish is the result of suffering a long, incurable illness, terminating that life deliberately is forbidden to a Muslim.

No matter how ill a person may be, or how distressed, they should try to bear it with patience and not beg Allah to be allowed to die. Many times human nature cries out because of suffering; it may be that all one's friends or loved ones have already gone, and there seems to be nothing left. However, the person does not know in what ways Allah is using their example as an aid to others, and death will always come when Allah wishes it. Even though the illness or death seems such a terrible tragedy, other good things arise out of it, and blessings will be given to make up for the suffering.

Umm Salamah recorded that the Messenger ﷺ said: 'If any Muslim who suffers some calamity says what Allah has commanded—'We belong to Allah and to Allah we shall return; O Allah, reward me for any affliction, give me something better in exchange for it'—then Allah will give something better in exchange: (Muslim 1999).

It is better to pray for strength and courage, and to try to develop inner peace, and accept that Allah will grant death to an individual when it is 'better' for him or her.

Anas recorded: 'None of you should wish for death for any calamity that befalls you, but should say: 'O Allah! Cause me to live so long as life is better for me; and cause me to die when death is better for me.' (Abu Dawud 3102, Bukhari 70.19.575).People may argue that modern medical technology can prolong a patient's life *artificially*. What has to be considered here is the definition of life, and how it is prolonged. If what is meant is that people whose bodies are artificially kept going on life-supporting machines would die once the machine is switched off, then that is a special case. If the brain of such a person has actually ceased to function, then the life of that person has ended, even though the heart may continue to beat with the help of the machine. Here, we are not really speaking about euthanasia, but about the definition of whether or not life still exists in a person. The out-of-body experiences of people on their death-beds indicate that the souls have already left and may well be watching the whole scene from some other vantage point.[1]

The use of life-support machines is highly beneficial if it gives doctors a breathing space to administer a treatment which will ensure that the patient recovers. If it is clear that the patient's brain has died, and there is no way to bring him or her back to life, there is no benefit in the machinery; the switching off in these cases does not therefore fall into the category of euthanasia—it is merely letting a natural course take its effect.

The notions of killing somebody in order to give them 'the right to die with dignity' or 'sparing the patient unbearable pain' are understandable but misguided. It is quite wrong to suggest that a person struggling with pain or illness lacks dignity; they deserve all possible help, and to speak of euthanasia in these cases is really a condemnation of a modern society that is unwilling to help adequately. With the advances in medicine, pain which used to be considered unbearable is now much relieved or controlled. Muslims should try not to rant and rave against God or their unpleasant circumstances. One important cheering factor to keep in mind is that when they bear their pains without losing faith, it is not pointless suffering, but it will be counted for them towards the

---

1. Reports from people who have gone through this experience suggest how many of them were very impatient and indignant at the treatment meted out to their vacated bodies, and were very happy to move on to the next stage of existence and did not wish to be held back).

forgiveness of their sins.

Umm al-Ala recorded that the Apostle ﷺ visited her when she was sick. He said: 'Be glad, Umm al-Ala, for Allah removes the sins of a Muslim for his (or her) illness, as fire removes the dross from gold and silver.' (Abu Dawud 3086).

Aishah recorded that she told the Apostle of Allah ﷺ that the most severe verse in the Qur'an was: 'If anyone does evil, he will be requited for it.' He said: 'Do you know, Aishah that when a believer is afflicted with a calamity or a thorn, it serves as an atonement for his evil deed.' (Abu Dawud 3087, Bukhari 70.1.544).

Abu Said al-Khudri and Abu Hurayrah recorded: 'No fatigue, nor disease, nor sorrow, nor sadness, nor hurt, nor distress befall a Muslim, even if it were (as small as) the prick of a thorn, but Allah expiates some of his (or her) sins for it.' (Bukhari 70.1.545).

A POSITIVE ATTITUDE, PRAYER AND MEDICAL HELP

The Blessed Prophet ﷺ took a very positive attitude when visiting sick people whoever they were, and at any stage of their illness. He expected Allah to hear his petition, and heal the sick one, if his or her time had not yet come. He also expected other people's prayers to be heard too. The sick could find renewed strength and courage from the prayer-support of those that cared for them.

Ibn Amr recorded: 'When a person comes to visit a sick person, he (or she) should say: 'O Allah! Cure

Your servant, who may then wreak havoc on an enemy in Your cause, or walk at a funeral for your sake.' (Abu Dawud 3101).

Ibn Abbas recorded the Prophet ﷺ as saying: 'If anyone visits a sick person whose time (of death) has not yet come, and says with him seven times: ' I ask Allah, the Almighty, the Lord of the Mighty Throne, to cure you!' then Allah will cure him (or her) from that disease.' (Abu Dawud 3100).

Some people wonder how one can reconcile praying for the cure of a sick person with the belief that everything that has happened is God's will. They wonder whether it might acutally be a lack of faith to pray for health. If it is God's will, for some reason known only to Him, for that person to be ill, or to die, then what is the point of anyone praying that they may be made better?

We have to think about two things. Firstly, a very great number of people pray desperately for healing for themselves or their loved ones, and it is *not* granted. They receive no miraculous cure no matter how saintly their lives may have been; the person remains ill, or perhaps dies. Does this mean that God does not care about that person, or enjoys the spectacle of watching them suffer and waste away? By no means—God is with us in every bit of our suffering.

On the other hand, we have the example of many of the famous prophets who successfully prayed for healing, and some who even prayed for a dead person who was then raised to life. Three such raisings are recorded of the Blessed Jesus صلى الله عليه وسلم, for example, and many, many healings. The Blessed Prophet Muhammad صلى الله عليه وسلم was in complete accord with healing prayer and practised it regularly for his family and friends, and anyone who requested his help.

We can only assume from this, therefore, that no matter how illogical it might seem to a theological brain, it was quite in keeping with the will of Allah for such prayers to be made; and there must have been enough positive results to these prayers for them to be have been considered worthwhile.

Therefore, it is correct practice for a Muslim to exercise his or her compassion in praying for the healing of another, and to do their utmost to bring about that other person's restoration to health and happiness.

However, having faith in Allah is not to be regarded as being in any way contrary to the desire to seek medical help and make use of medical expertise as well. The two—faith and medicine—go hand-in-hand. There is no virtue whatsoever in refusing to accept medical treatment stubbornly believing this to be lacking in faith!

Usamah ibn Sharik said: 'I came to the Prophet صلى الله عليه وسلم and his companions were sitting (as still as) if they had birds on their heads. I saluted and sat down. Desert Arabs were coming from here and there, and asking: 'Apostle of Allah, should we make use of medical treatment?' He replied, '(Yes), make use of medical treatment, for Allah has not created a disease without also creating a remedy for it, with the exception of one disease (only)—namely, old age!' (Abu Dawud 3846).

Obviously, as Creator, Allah is ultimately responsible for the existence of sickness and disease on this planet—it was He who created the microbes and bacteria that surround us continually in the air we breathe and in the substances we eat and drink.

However, the Blessed Prophet ﷺ was quite clear that Allah had provided everything necessary on this planet to deal with sickness or poison caused by other natural substances, and intended these things to be used.

'Abu al-Darda recorded that the Prophet ﷺ stated quite clearly: 'Allah has sent down both the disease and the cure, and He has appointed a cure for every disease; so treat yourselves medically, but use nothing unlawful.' (Abu Dawud 3865, see also Bukhari 71.1.582).

The only times the Prophet ﷺ did not approve of using medicine was when the remedy contained haram substances—for example, pork or alcohol. (He also mentioned medicine prepared from frogs (Abu Dawud 3862)—but this is an unlikely prescription these days!)

Abu Hurayrah recorded: 'The Apostle of Allah ﷺ forbade unclean medicine.' (Abu Dawud 3861).

Wail recorded that Tariq ibn Suwaid asked the Prophet ﷺ about wine (used in medicine), and he forbade it. He asked him again, and he (again) forbade him. He said to him: 'Prophet of Allah, it is a medicine!' The Prophet ﷺ said: 'No, it is a disease!' (Abu Dawud 3864).

It is important to bear this in mind when having prescriptions made up by the modern doctors or chemists, for many medicines have alcohol bases, or may include animal fats or use gelatine from animals killed in a haram manner. However, the rule of necessity applies here—a rule often overlooked by extreme zealots. The rule is that if no halal food is available, in the circumstances one may eat haram and not be held at fault. Likewise, when considering medicines, if the malady is a serious matter and there is nothing else available, then a medicine with haram contents may be taken—but it is highly commendable to press the medical authorities for more research into medicine with non-alcohol bases, for there are substitutes available.

CONCLUSION

By the grace of Him in whose hands are all our souls, let us all learn to love each other and be more tolerant of our various shortcomings, praying to our Lord to forgive us our weaknesses and failures, and bring us the strength to regain our strong faith in Him. Let us try to bring light out of darkness, and to find new hope and a renewed sense of love for others out of experience of suffering loss and bereavement. In the name of Him who is the Compassionate, the Merciful One. Amen.

Chapter 7

Anger

One aspect of the distress of bereavement is that
neither the love for the lost person nor the
mourners who are doing the loving are perfect.
Instead of accepting the will of Allah the bereaved
often experience some self-hate, self-accusation and
guilt.

The anger and hostility may take quite irrational
forms. It can be directed against the medical people
who looked after the deceased, the nearest and dearest, and the dead people themselves—the ones who
have caused the bereaved so much distress by dying
and therefore abandoning them!

Many of the anger feelings are quite understandable. The mourner is thinking—'How could you give
up and desert me with all these problems, children,
etc.?' 'You were so foolish!' 'Why didn't you go to the
doctor before?' 'How many times did I warn you that
you should take more care of yourself, stop smoking,
etc?' 'I could kill you for the pain/mess you've caused
me.' 'God, how could you let an innocent child die?'
'Why am I being punished like this when I've done
nothing wrong?'

Ask any grieving person directly if they are angry

with the deceased, they will automatically deny it. It is not done to speak ill of the dead. Two relevant sayings of the Prophet ﷺ are recorded, one by Aishah: 'When your companion dies, leave him and do not revile him' (Abu Dawud 4881), and one by Ibn 'Umar: 'Speak of the virtues of your dead, and refrain from mentioning their evils' (Abu Dawud 4882).

Reviling the dead is more serious than reviling the living for there is no chance to later beg pardon of them when you have calmed down. If they did sin, then they will have the punishment for their sins, and it is pointless for you to revile and abuse them further. In any case, it may be that Allah will forgive their sins, whatever you may feel about them.

Mourners are very shocked and afraid of this sudden upsurge of anger in themselves, and it adds to their guilt. They know they shouldn't be thinking like this. It seems very disrespectful towards the dead. Once again, if they can be brought to realise that this is also a natural part of their mourning, and almost universal, they will be less afraid of their emotions and forgive themselves in due course. A kind helper could ask gently what it is the bereaved miss about their lost ones; then ask what they do *not* miss a few times.

There is one serious danger in anger. Often, in times of great stress such as coping with death, people may be afraid of letting their anger explode outward, so they turn it against themselves, bringing about the state of clinical depression as the result. Sometimes they even believe that they really cannot go on without the lost one, and contemplate suicide. This may actually be a way of saying 'I am so angry at myself that I must punish myself!' The self has laid upon itself the 'duty' of being its own executioner.

When anger becomes intolerable to the individual, the consequences may be serious indeed. Anger has to be admitted, analysed, acted out and abandoned— and the hardest thing is probably admitting it. We must lift it up to objective examination. Why am I so upset? Does my behaviour or attitude make sense? The kind helper encourages the mourner to back off and look at the anger—realise where it comes from. It can be a weak spot in personality—it is not worth what it causes in inner stress or fractured human relationships. If possible, it should be abandoned for insight, understanding and healthy action.

Let us take one simple example—the burden of 'keeping up appearances'. This is quite a severe task, especially for a man trying to maintain those emotions and feelings he has been brought up to believe are 'manly' and right. There is a common fallacious belief that men are only fully masculine when they perform roles that show them to be active, in pursuit of definable goals. A truly masculine man is most at home in the external world of action. He pays a price for this mis-belief, for when he finds himself confronted by the internal world of thought and emotion, he feels lost, ill at ease, on 'foreign ground', The deeper he is drawn in to his emotions, the more he feels his masculinity is endangered.

Such a man can suffer dreadful agonies of hurt and remorse when a wife or child dies, perhaps because he regards women and children as weaker than himself, and feels that he has failed to protect those in his care. If a wife or child dies, some men go further, and angrily accuse God of failing them, for neither they nor God were able to protect their loved ones.

This is a neurosis, and not Islam. If you think about it, it is a way of challenging and complaining about the will of God—who knew from the moment of the conception in the womb of that loved one the exact moment when their souls would leave their bodies. 'Nor can a soul die except by God's leave, the term being fixed as by writing.' (3:145); 'When their time expires, they would not be able to delay (it) for a single hour, just as they will not be able to anticipate it (for a single hour) (16:61).

There is no point whatsoever in fretting about this—the decision concerning the length of one's time-span here is always fixed and known by God, no matter how much it may catch us humans by surprise. 'They ask you about the Hour—when will be its appointed time? Say: 'The knowledge of it is with my Lord (alone); none but He can reveal as to when it will occur' (7:187). We are not given to know the reasons why certain things happen in our lives, or the time-schedules for them.

Sometimes we get very upset by what happens, but then, we should sit down and try to raise our thoughts to a higher level, in which we see from a wider viewpoint that if God takes away a loved one it is for a reason. We are not being tested to see if we can continue to grieve and think about nothing else but our loss for the rest of our own lives. To lay down our grief is not disloyalty to the dead loved one, but acceptance of a higher plan.

However, the reaction of anger is accepted by many men, and understood—because anger and desire for revenge are 'manly'; grief is not merely thought to be 'womanly' but also an abdication of responsibility. To 'give way' to tears and grief is to suffer a loss of masculinity. Some masculine men actually feel fear if they let themselves 'give in' to grief. They think that if they do this they will be overwhelmed, paralysed, emasculated, unable to keep control.

These fears and assumptions are not based on a rational, thought-out response to the world as it is. They are not being logical—but it is no use asking why a man should feel less masculine if he cries; the fact is, he does, and will try to stop crying as soon as he can. He will try to 'master' his emotions.

As it happens, anger has quite an important function in the mourning process of many people. If they have gone numb inside and shut out all their emotions, it is anger which often breaks through the numbness and denial, and so frees the person who was locked up inside their own loss.

The price men pay for being protective citadels is that it becomes risky for them to admit having vulnerable emotions like fear, grief, sense of failure, longing for something or someone irrevocably lost, misery, loneliness, etc. Helplessness attacks a man's deepest assumptions about who he is, his maleness, what makes him valuable. The most effective way he sometimes finds of dealing with the problem is simply to pretend and convince himself that it doesn't exist.

Denial, however, is only a short-term method of coping with trauma. When a person has suffered physical injury, the body sometimes copes by denying pain that is too excrutiating to bear. It goes into shock, the body's first line of defence. Sometimes a badly injured person does not feel pain for quite a long time. But eventually the pain returns, and it has a specific function—it indicates the place and nature of the injury. If we didn't have the pain, we wouldn't know how to set about the process of mending the injury. Emotional trauma is very similar—the person who has lost a partner, child, (or things like home or job), needs just as much ease and protection as if they'd been knocked down by a car. They need peace, calm and attention, so that their healing process can begin.

If a badly injured person insists on limping off, asserting that nothing is wrong, you'd say he was in shock and that this deception wouldn't last. Sometimes, after death, people suppress and deny their grief symptoms, and force this denial to become their way of life. They may think that everyone around them will applaud this way of behaving, and so believe that the best way of dealing with their 'injury' is to forget it for good.

This behaviour is actually not brave, nor commendable; it is stupid. You cannot lead life as usual if you have a broken leg. Nor can you lead life as usual with a broken heart. The real problem for all injured people is getting better, and you can only do this if you allow the injury to heal. The healing can only begin to happen after you acknowledge in faith that you have been hurt.

Chapter 8

Guilt

There is also a great deal of suffering caused by guilt—guilt about what was said or not said, done or not done, justified guilt, and guilt with no rational justification. The guilt may be the result of very genuine regrets about insufficient care or concern, or it may be based on fantasy. In fact, our guilt is usually a mixture of realistic and unrealistic aspects.

Mourners may feel guilty because they believe they failed their loved ones on their deathbeds. They intended to pray with them, and stay at their side while they died, but when it came to it could not face it and fled the room; or perhaps they left the room briefly for some perfectly justifiable reason, and it was during those few moments that the loved one died. We dwell on what we might have done differently; and this indicates that we have not yet abandoned the mental hope that the death is irreversible.

'I went away, I went and left you.' 'I was weak, frightened, couldn't bear it—so I left you alone.' 'I did not do my duty.' 'I did not say the right words.'

The mourner may feel guilty for not having told the dying ones of impending death, and thus depriving them of any preparation for it. They might feel guilty for neglecting them, not loving them enough, not giving them enough strength until it was too late. Maybe they became impatient or distressed, and wished that the dying ones would die quickly, and 'get it over with' and then—to their horror—they did.

Devoted mourners may suffer excruciating guilt for very trivial reasons—if only they had not said that particular phase, or argued yesterday; if only they had arrived a little earlier, sent the letter, telephoned; if only they had persuaded the wife to go to the doctors earlier, or to a different doctor! Some feel guilty because they feel they should be grieving more, or differently. Usually they are criticising themselves quite unreasonably. A kind helper could ask them to describe all the things they actually *did*. This helps to restore perspective.

When a loved one dies, we will *always* be able to find something we wish we had done differently, something to blame ourselves for. We are human beings, not robots, and human beings do fail. If we demand perfection of ourselves and our relationship with the patient we shall probably give far less than if we can relax and accept that if everyone does the best they can, that is sufficient, and no failure is final—with God.

Allah not only forgives our failures, He sees our successes where no-one else does, not even we ourselves. Only God can give us credit for the angry words we did not speak, temptations we resisted, patience and gentleness little noticed and long forgotten by those around us. Such good deeds are never wasted nor forgotten, because God gives them a measure of eternity.

'Whatever good you send forth for your souls before you, you will find it with God. For God sees all that you do.' (2:110).

'Who is he (or she) that will lend to God a beautiful loan, which God will double to his (or her) credit, and multiply many times?' (2:111).

'.....God suffers not the reward to be lost of any who do good—nor could they spend anything, small or great, nor cut across a valley, but their deed is inscribed to their credit, that God may requite their deed with the best possible reward.' (9:120-121).

'O believers! Fear God, and let every soul look to what (provision) he (or she) has sent forth for the morrow.' (59:18).

All the wrong we have ever done can be forgiven and forgotten if we are willing to bring it to Allah. It is never too late to find peace with Allah, or to make peace with those we have wronged.

'If anyone does evil or wrongs his (or her) own soul, but afterwards seeks God's forgiveness, he (or she) will find God Oft-Forgiving, Most Merciful.' (4:110).

It is important for the mourner to be released from unnecessary burdens of guilt. Maybe you could suggest that they take the opportunity to return in their

imagination to the death-bed and do something different. Confront it again, and this time, be able to say
farewell. In fact, if you believe in the afterlife of your
loved one, then this is not a silly thing to do—the loved
one will understand perfectly all that you intended to
do. It should console a mourner considerably to realise
that the dying one understood all along, and was
grateful for everything done on their behalf, even if
they never had the chance to say so.

Don't feel guilty! Don't forget, often mourners are
already in a state of shock when the death of their
loved one occurs. If you like, you could talk to that
departed one as if they were still there, able to hear
you. Tell them everything you wished you had said—
that you love them and wanted to say goodbye. Weep
and sob like a helpless child, and do not feel ashamed.
Then feel the loss which you were keeping at bay.

At a later stage, some mourners find themselves
feeling guilty when they at last begin to recapture the
sense of life and joy and growth. They feel they are
'letting down' the dead one by abandoning their deep
mourning. This is a terrible and tragic mistake. They
are not letting the dead loved one down at all. Look at
it the other way round. Just because someone you love
has died does not mean that they have stopped loving
you, and if they are aware of your too-great grief while
at the same time unable to do anything to console you,
this must cause *them* pain. Try to think of it that way
round. Your dead loved one would wish you to pick
yourself up, and be able to enjoy the rest of your life.

Your dead loved one would not wish you to become helpless, or ill, or bitter, or paralysed emotionally.

On the same topic, it is quite wrong for other people to add to the struggles of a mourner by deliberately trying to make them feel guilty when they are beginning to come out of their grief. Instead, they should be helping them back to life!

On occasions, of course, a mourner did behave very badly to the deceased. In these cases, they sometimes find relief for their guilt by devoting their lives to paying restitution. Someone who was 'hated' during their lifetime suddenly becomes cherished, a 'saint', very special, very important, someone who never did any wrong. What is happening is that the mourner is idealising the deceased—the false claims of the deceased's 'saintliness' are really attempts on the part of guilty mourners at restitution, a defence against the pain of their guilt.

Most mourners, out of respect for the dead, idealise their deceased to a certain extent, which may reinforce the denial of real feeling and the memory of a real relationship. The dead person suddenly becomes 'too good to be true'. A useful question to help bring the mourner back to reality is—'what don't you miss about that person?'

A recognition of the universality of this need to idealise may help any Muslim mourner who shows exaggerated responses. If they can be made to see that most mourners go through this stage, then maybe they will start to forgive themselves, and accept reality. If they can then be helped to see the lost ones not only with all the loved and admired aspects of their personalities but also with the irritating and feared ones, the 'warts and all,' then the exaggerated mourning and idealisation may become modified, and the bereaved may become able to see that they still loved them, even in spite of their faults!

To be able to feel guilt is not bad, but a gift of Allah. It is a sign of our capacity to feel with others. If we do something that hurts, we can feel the hurt. Throughout the years as we grow towards adulthood there is a build-up of this capacity, and this is healthy and important. Our whole system of law and order is founded on the assumption that human beings are creatures capable of feeling guilt, and that guilt usually keeps them from injuring others or violating their rights.

There are at least three different kinds of guilt involved with bereavement. There is real guilt, where somebody really has done something to regret, and the cause-and-effect relationships are obvious. In these cases, the mourner really has let the deceased down in some way, and they know it. They cannot turn the clock back and put it right, so they suffer guilt as the inevitable result.

Secondly, there is neurotic guilt. This is where the guilt effect is out of all proportion to the cause, and its origin is largely in the tormented mind of the bereaved person. The mourner is feeling much more of the painful emotion than is warranted by the circumstances. There is an impulse here to self-punishment.

Thirdly, there is existential guilt, which is so deeply implanted in life that cause-and-effect seem to be irrelevant—this guilt is felt because an individual is trapped in a generally poor opinion of his or her capacities, not because of any particular act or event.

We can see an example of neurotic guilt when somebody who can ill afford it insists on burying a relative with a very expensive or ornate gravestone, or organises costly 'funeral parties' or 'remembrance services'. It is too late to make amends to the deceased directly, so the guilty party does the next best thing and punishes the wallet, and thereby discharges the personal obligation. It is as if they were openly pleading guilty of neglect and asking for a fine.

It is significant that all these sorts of extravagances are disapproved of in Islam. The grave of the deceased should not be made into a shrine, but should be a simple place where the body of the loved one can be laid with respect, and remembered as they really were. (See p. 147, 150).

Chapter 9

Fear and Forgiveness

It is human to be afraid, and nothing to be guilty about. It has nothing to do with sin or doing wrong. Fear is a sign that we are alive, and that our brains are working. Without it we are probably suffering from a physical or mental handicap. It is a signal that danger is near. We need to feel fear. If we refuse to notice fears, we begin to allow them to dictate how we behave. This will lead us to become confused and divided inside, and go on to produce forms of anger and violence. What is wrong is for a Muslim to be controlled or driven by their fears.

> 'Whosoever follows My guidance, on them shall be no fear, neither shall they grieve.' (2:38).

> 'Whoever submits their whole self to Allah and is a doer of good—they will get their reward with their Lord. On such shall be no fear, neither shall they grieve.' (2:112. See also 10:62).

Unacknowledged fear is dangerous, and like nuclear waste, it cannot be disposed of; it can only be stored. It goes on acting and developing in destructive ways. Facing fears means facing facts, and facing the

truth can be uncomfortable, but it does slowly release
the grip of fear. We have to face the truth in order to
stop pretending, deceiving ourselves and other people.

Acknowledging fear is not easy, especially if we
condemn it in others or regard it as a sign of failure in
ourselves. 'Big boys don't cry,' 'Muslims should not be
afraid.' We receive this impression in youth and grow
up believing it to be true.

But big boys do cry and Muslims are afraid. Yes,
maybe the ideal is someone who is self-sufficient,
independent, reliable, mature—no weaknesses; but
we should not forget that even the Blessed Muhammad
ﷺ was a man who cried.

> 'Do you think that you will enter the Garden
> without such (trials) as came to those who
> passed away before you? They encountered
> suffering and adversity, and were so shaken
> in spirit that even the Messenger and those of
> faith who were with him cried: 'When (will
> come) the help of Allah?' Ah, Truly, the help of
> Allah is near!' (2:214).

Much suffering can be caused by falsely insisting
that it is impossible for Muslims to be afraid. 'Be sure
that We will test you with something of fear' said Allah
(2:155). This does not mean that we will lose confidence in Allah, or that we will not be brave. The
bravest people in the world are those who get on with
whatever it is they have to do, even though they might
be terrified! If we cry and feel fear, we are not failing,
we are simply being human, like the messenger of our
faith. What matters to the Muslim is how we react to

our fear, how we face up to it and tackle it.

Acknowledging fears becomes easier when we begin to realise that certain fears are universal to all human beings—so we can hardly be blamed for having them. Once we can realise that we are not special or different, we can stop expecting ourselves to be 'super-human'. Let us be honest—keeping up the pretence of freedom from fear is exhausting and inwardly painful, like having somebody stick pins in our legs under the table while we have to pretend all is well, and not show anything on our faces.

Since we are not perfect, we have so many fears that Islam can help to put in perspective—fear of failing people's expectations; fear of losing dignity by admitting we need help; fear of criticism and disapproval, and of losing our reputation. When we develop fear of losing control, or of involvement with others, we begin to isolate ourselves. We develop an island mentality, and surround ourselves with a sea of loneliness.

We put up the facade of independence, and begin to believe in our own pretence. Because of our pride, we begin to believe that we are self-sufficient, and become increasingly unable to acknowledge what we can and do receive from others.

This self-inflicted isolation causes us to appear aloof or shy, and people begin to believe that we do not want to be approached at all; and so our loneliness and fear of losing control increases all the more.

Sharing our fears with anyone is risky—we risk

rejection. Our listener may judge us and desert us, and in our wounded state we dread being cut off and excluded. It takes real determination to find someone to trust and confide in. Making friends is an adventure and takes courage. It is dangerous because it involves trust, openness and love, and if trust is betrayed then openness turns to cynicism, and love can turn into hatred and rejection. The fear of betrayal, cynicism and rejection often prevents us from even attempting the art of friendship, so we allow ourselves to be caught in this wretched cycle of fear. In effect, we create our own isolation and deny any possibility of being comforted, healed or helped by a friend.

For the Muslim, the tragedy of a person's death is not the end of the story. Muslims are taught from birth to have confidence that there is life after death. Therefore it seems to many Muslims quite illogical to grieve the loss of someone who has simply left this earth and gone on to other things. This is theoretically true, but even while believing in the life to come, it is still unhealthy to skip too quickly over the feelings of loss and tragedy that bereaved people experience.

We shall feel a sense of loss, and an acheing void, if we have been close to the person who has died. We need to acknowledge those feelings in ourselves and in other people. It is part of acknowledging the whole truth.

This is one reason why funerals are so important— they are times when we give each other the opportunity to grieve and also to express our faith in God and the future life. Death can then be transformed, very gently, from tragedy to triumph.

If we don't talk about our fear of death we deprive not only ourselves but also our children of a healthy facing of reality.They will grow up unprepared for loss. It is more helpful when there is no pretence or camouflage. Losing precious things does hurt. Facing death is about facing loss. We have to learn how to regard our bodies as God's, and be prepared to give them back when He wants them.

Once we have found the courage to confront our fears, and share them with another person, we begin to feel more alive. The paralysis that has gripped us gradually lets go and life returns. We begin to face the future with new energy.

Fear of death stalks us until we accept that this is part of what it means to be alive. We need to discover how to live the short span that we have to the fullest extent. This only really becomes fully possible after we have been 'touched' by death.

Allah knows that we are human. Our fears are not signs of disobedience or sin which need to be punished, but human frailties which need understanding and compassion. Muslims who feel that they have to apologise for being afraid, often go on to believe that they are not good enough, and Allah will not accept them. This craving for perfection is actually unhealthy and damaging—and challenges the will of God who was pleased to create us human. Learning to accept ourselves as God accepts us is a very difficult lesson for some! It seems incredible that God should find us acceptable, loved even, just as we are, with all our imperfections—so long as our intention is Islam.

Sometimes religious people develop a neurotic guilt which leads to a very peculiar 'cosmic fantasy'—they believe that God is deliberately manoeuvring painful events in order to punish them for their misdeeds. It is quite common to hear people gasp 'Why did God do this to me?' This attitude distorts the basic structure of the universe in a way that makes a person doubly vulnerable to the crises of life. At a time when a friendly cosmic force is most needed, God may become an enemy!

Islam teaches that although painful events may well occur as the result of our sinfulness, cruelty, selfishness or neglect, the fate of one person is NOT a means of punishing another.

'Every soul draws the reward of its acts on none but itself; no bearer of burdens can bear the burden of another.' (6:164).

'On no soul does God place a burden greater than it can bear. It gets every good that it earns and suffers every ill that it earns.' (2:286).

'Guard yourself against a Day when one soul shall not avail another, nor shall compensation be accepted from her, nor shall intercession profit her, nor shall anyone be helped.' (2:123).

No human being can pass through this life without hurt or loss.

> 'Be sure that We shall test you with something
> of fear and hunger, some loss of goods or lives
> or the fruits (of your toil); but give glad tidings
> to those who patiently persevere and say,
> when afflicted with calamity: To God we
> belong, and to Him is our return.' (2:155-156).

No person is immune to biological bacteria, or the laws of gravity, etc. We live in a world of natural laws, of cause and effect, and sadly—no matter how much we might fantasise and wish it were so—if someone fires a bullet at our head, it is unlikely that God will miraculously intervene and catch the bullet. If the Muslim accepts that the time span of life is fixed, then what appears to be a miraculous avoidance of certain death is not really a miracle at all. Muslims know that they will not die before their 'time'.

Allah is the Compassionate, the Merciful. He sees all our failings and weaknesses, and still loves us. He waits only for us to turn to Him and express our sorrow at our inadequacies—and He forgives us. Punishment is not the fate of weak mortals who are sorry, but those so hardened by their lives of sin that they refuse to repent. Sending someone to Hell is never of God's choosing, always the fault of the one who denies.

Sometimes those who have always been 'righteous' get very annoyed with God for His generous benevolence towards the penitent weak ones; they cannot bear the thought of sinners 'cheating' their deserved punishment—but this is not Islam.

The Qur'an states quite plainly that 'if God punished us according to what we deserved, there would not remain on earth one living thing.' (16:61). Thankfully, Allah is our Judge, and not any of the human righteous!.

Talking about forgiveness, Allah knew we would not be perfect, and that we would hurt one another. He knew that there are ways of changing our behaviour to be more loving rather than less loving; to be more accepting rather than less so, and to be more creative and less destructive. But He left us to choose which way we want to go. The Blessed Apostle of God ﷺ did not moralise or repeat multitudes of commandments— he lived a certain way. He showed us the kind of life that God would like us to follow.

> 'You have indeed in the Messenger of Allah a beautiful pattern, for anyone whose hope is in God and the Final Day, and who engages much in the praise of God.' (33:21).

As Aishah once stated of her dear husband, 'His way of life is the Qur'an!'

He showed us that God loves and accepts us as He made us, and stays with us through suffering, even through deliberate wrong-doing or sin, helping us to learn to practise forgiveness and to change our ways, becoming more loving human beings.

'A man said of another, 'By Allah, Allah will never forgive him!' At this Allah the Almighty said—'Who is this who swears by Me that I will never forgive a certain person? Truly, I have forgiven him already.'

'O son of man, so long as you call upon Me and ask

of Me. I shall forgive you for what you have done.'
(Hadith Qudsi, Ezzedine Ibrahim, Beirut, 1980).

With God there is no ulterior motive, no strings
attached. He loves us with a pure love that has no wish
to dominate, manipulate, or coerce. There is no com-
pulsion in His pure love. He loves, He waits, and
leaves us to respond when we are ready—and He goes
on loving, whatever our response.

Unconditional love, or grace, is not like an
anaesthetic, imposing a false sense that pain has ceased.
It helps us *in* our infirmities, *while* we are suffering, *during* the times of great fear, to face what is happening.
Grace comes to help in time of need. Allah does not remove the storm, He helps us in the midst of the storm.

When we harden our hearts it is often because we
have been hurt or felt threatened. If we feel hurt or
betrayed by someone who is either dying or has died,
we have the choice either to harden our hearts or to
forgive. Choosing to forgive is vital for wholeness. It
makes all the difference to whether we blossom and
flourish, growing healthy and loving, or whether we
grow into bitter, withered and twisted people who
gradually lose the capacity for living a full and reward-
ing life. The hurt we felt will turn to anger, and we will
begin to hurt other people in return, contributing to a
destructive way of life.

Being forgiven is part of the same process, and just
as difficult. If we are aware only of forgiving, it implies
that we can never hurt people and have no reason to
receive forgiveness ourselves. This makes us

patronising and aloof, unaware of what holds us together. If the person we have hurt has died, then we have to confess our failings to God and allow Him to forgive us; and forgive ourselves!

Nothing is more pathetic than the person who runs out of life before he is dead. Forgiveness of others releases us and gives us peace—and that is a prime factor in any healing. But we have to recognise that there are also times when forgiving others is not enough; we also have to forgive ourselves—and we sometimes find that even harder to do. We may state that we believe God freely forgives all our wrong if we confess it and ask for His forgiveness, but we do not let go of the guilt. We keep it like a stick to beat ourselves with, because unconditional forgiveness seems too much like an easy option.

We must fully and completely accept and embrace His forgiveness and love. Guilt feelings and inferiority before God are expressions of selfishness, or self-centredness; by clinging on to them we give greater importance to our little sinful self than to His immense and never-ending love. We must surrender our guilt and inferiority to Him; His goodness is greater than our badness.

The peace that comes through this forgiveness brings healing and acceptance to the bereaved, and it is very important. There are persons who shape their lives by the fear of death, and persons who shape their lives by the joy of life. The former live dying, the latter die living.

Chapter 10

Grief and Religion

Does a person's religion make any difference to the way they experience death and grief? It depends on their understanding of religion, even Islam. There are healthy attitudes to religion, and there are unhealthy ones. Unfortunately, while it is certainly a fact that some religious attitudes help the personality to grow, others seriously stunt it.

Unhealthy religion is usually centred about the denial of responsibility. It projects a concept of a God who is capricious and open to manipulation. Believers with this sort of attitude often act rather like spoiled children; they seem to genuinely believe that if they cry loudly enough or long enough they will be able to bring themselves to God's attention, make Him notice their worthy cause, and perhaps even make Him act differently—in accordance with what they want Him to do. They seem to expect that if they are devoted enough, or chant enough phrases, or do enough pious practices, Allah will produce cosmic results and violate the law and order of the universe just to oblige them.

All their prayers and incantations might seem

very pious, but their attitude is really one of subtle shirk, and certainly one of lack of trust in the will of Allah. God does not need to be told our problems—He knows everything already. He will not have failed to observe that one of His servants is sick, or dying, or bereaved.

But God is not there just to oblige us—no matter how worthy we are, or how desperate our cause. God is not a cosmic errand-boy. He is not standing by, waiting for our 'orders of the day'—sometimes with the implication that He had better get on with doing what we want Him to do or we will punish Him by rejecting Him. This is a real trivialisation of the nature of God, and yet we find so frequently examples of people who lose their 'faith' in God because He did not do what they wanted Him to do—He let their loved one die.

It is good for a Muslim to be reminded that no person was more righteous or more loved by Allah than the Blessed Apostle Muhammad ﷺ—and yet there was no miraculous cure for his sickness, and he died, as all humans must die. Remember how his companion Umar could not bring himself to accept his death, and how Abu Bakr took command by reminding them of the *ayah*:

> 'Muhammad is but a messenger; there have
> been prophets before him, and they all died.
> Will you now turn back?' (3:144).

True religion enables us to take charge of our own

lives and accept responsibilty in a disciplined way, and this reduces the causes of guilt and sets in motion wise processes necessary for the management of grief.

Some bereaved people feel that they are so helpless to cope with life that they need a special dole of 'cosmic kindness' to get them through. Muslims do not need to crawl through life begging for what is already theirs—God's love and caring concern. They know their duty is towards Him. They have to stand in faith, and accept His will.

While they may not like the results of a molecular process when someone succumbs to disease, or the impersonal results of the law of gravity when a wall falls on an innocent bystander, or the war that follows from the political failures of people over whom we have no control but who can devastate our lives, they would not want to destroy reality by asking God to act in a way that would entail a violation of His nature. We cannot tempt God to do our will. It is important instead to discover how to bring our lives into close accord with His will.

Death seen in terms of a capricious universe with a God who should do our bidding is painful and depressing; death contemplated when we understand the meaning of life in a larger context is seen in a totally different light. It may be that life is as short as a moth's, or as long as a sequoia tree's; what matters is not its length but its quality.

Our religious faith should help us find a perspective through which we can evaluate our own feelings.

Healthy religion moves beyond the denial of responsibility, the distortion of reality and the creating of illusions. It puts death in perspective. It helps us to understand the meaning of the pain that comes with some death and is absent in others. It undergirds life with an adequate philosophy, emphasizes the reality of life, and the forms of love that continue to sustain life.

Only physical things die; spiritual things already have the dimension of the infinite and eternal and are therefore indestructible.

Death tosses the human being into spiritual turmoil. One of the biggest problems for devout believers is the attitude of so many friends, who—because of their sincere faith in the afterlife—simply do not seem to see that there is a problem in a person's grief; or if they do see it, they refuse to admit it.

'You are a committed Muslim; your family are committed Muslims. Muslims know there is nothing to fear about death—therefore we can all be quite sure that you will cope wonderfully with your grief and we need not worry about it.'

In reality, the mourner may *not* be coping very well with his or her grief, but because of the attitude of these pious 'comforters' cannot speak up or make it known that help is needed. In fact, religious people who speak like this are quite possibly trying to escape their own emotional involvement, which they find embarrassing or are unable to handle. Everyone feels inadequate, and lacks confidence in what to say for the best to a

bereaved person—and in fact, a companionable silence is often preferable to false platitudes.

Well? Should Muslims not grieve at all? Should
they just accept a terminal illness as God's will, or a test
of faith? What can they expect from God? What should
they ask Him for?

It is not wrong to ask questions. Human beings are
creatures with minds and rational faculties. If God had
wanted automatons with no minds, He would have
created us that way. It is all right for us to ask for the
reasons; but we cannot demand an answer. Sometimes
we get an answer, if God deems it necessary for us to
know. At other times we simply have to accept that
although there is an answer, God has not given it, and
since His dealings with us are always loving and for
our ultimate good, we can leave the matter there. This
is where faith comes in.

How does Islam affect Muslims? A life free from
guilt? Possibly, if they try hard. A life free from the fear
of death? Possibly, if they have enough faith. A life that
can be lived differently from that of non-believers?
True, with God's help. A life free from sorrow, problems and difficulties? Sadly, no.

> 'You shall certainly be tried and tested in your
> possessions and in your personal selves; and
> you shall certainly hear much that will dis-
> tress you, from those who received the Book
> before you, and from those who worship
> many gods. But if you persevere patiently,
> and guard against evil—then that will be the
> determining factor in everything.' (3:186).

Being a Muslim does not protect anyone from the reality of suffering. Belief is not some kind of spiritual inoculation which will provide immunity from all that is difficult and painful. We love Allah—but doesn't He care when we suffer? In times of crisis, it is so easy to feel that He is far away and cannot hear our cries—but this is not so. He is closer than our own neck vein; or, as the Messenger ﷺ touchingly put it, closer than the neck of our own camel. His love will never desert us or let us down, even in our darkest hour.

It is not wrong to grieve. People who believe in God grieve for all sorts of things, including the callous and hard-hearted attitudes some people have towards one another, and at the mess that human rebellion against God has made of His world. People with sympathetic hearts feel human misery deeply; some work to exhaustion to heal the sick and reach out to the needy. To see someone we love suffering makes us unutterably sad, and God knows that. He gave us the feelings in the first place.

But believers should not grieve in the same way as those who have no hope—for God promised His people comfort and strength right into the valley of the shadow of death, and beyond.

> 'Ibrahim said: 'O Lord! Show me how you give life to the dead.' He said: 'Do you not believe?' He said: 'Yes, but to satisfy my own understanding, (tell me).' Allah said: 'Take four birds and tame them to return to you; put one of them on each of four separate hills,

then call to them. They will come flying to you
with speed.' (2:260).

When Allah calls us, we will surely come flying to
Him. Our earthly life is the separation on the hills;
when we die, we will be called back to our real home,
with Allah.

'So do not lose heart, and do not fall into
despair; for you must gain mastery if you are
true in faith.' (3:139).

Many people wonder why, if God is all-powerful
and loving, He does not cure our loved ones of cancer,
or prevent wars and famines, etc—either directly
through miraculous intervention, or indirectly, perhaps through medical science.

God sometimes works through suffering. Some
people are physically healed, others are given the
ability to live with the illness and finally to die with
trust and hope. Suffering can never be considered
enjoyable, but there can be good responses to it. If we
can see that neither distress nor death can separate us
from the love of God we have a living hope which
transcends all the trials of our present situation.

As Muslims, who try to accept God's will, should
we fight the disease, or accept it? Would it be right for
a patient to refuse medical treatment on the grounds
that it must be God's will for them to have it? The
Muslim answer to that must surely be 'No'. Such
apathy is against the general desire of Allah to see us
always working for healing, wholeness and peace. We
have a responsibility to care for our bodies as best we

can—so we should encourage the patient to seek and take medical advice and co-operate with whatever treatment they think is right and is consistent with Islam; they should move towards full health as positively as they are able.

Human beings are required by Allah to seek medical treatment if it is available. The Prophet ﷺ himself told us to seek medical treatment; as he put it— 'Allah has not created an illness without creating a cure for it.' When you take a medicine, you are not acting against the will of Allah; you are cured *by* Allah's will, because He has put into that particular medicine the qualities which will enable the human body to overcome a certain disease.

Medicine functions by God's will. This is exactly what Umar ibn al-Khattab said to Abu Ubaydah once, when the latter questioned him about his orders concerning quarantine—preventing entry to or departure from an area where plague was widespread. Abu Ubaydah asked: 'Are we trying to escape from the will of Allah?' Umar answered: 'Yes, we try to escape from God's will with God's will.' This means that if we avoid certain causes of death we nevertheless remain subject to the will of Allah, because avoiding them and preventing them is also part of the will of Allah.

A Muslim will always have to acknowledge that the final outcome is in God's hands. If we pray du'a (personal prayer requests) for our sick and dying, and for the bereaved, it is never wasted; God always hears us, and something always 'happens', even if it not quite what the person has prayed for.

Umm Salamah the Prophet's 🖋 wife (peace be upon both of them) reported the Messenger 🖋 as saying: 'Whenever you visit the sick or the dying, make supplication for good, because the angels say 'Amen' to whatever you say.' (Muslim, 2002)

We are human and limited in our understanding. Instead of telling God what we want, we should try to ask God what it is He wants for us, or wants us to do, in each situation.

Sometimes He gives a very clear indication of what it is He wants us to do—through inner conviction, through a verse of the Qur'an, or an insight given through another person. When we are less certain, we can pray for what seems to be the best solution, acknowledging that God's wisdom is perfect.

We are not specks of dust drifting in space blown by random destiny. We are each of us unique—no two people are alike, not even identical twins. Each one of us is born for a specific reason and purpose, and each one of us will die when we have accomplished whatever it was to be accomplished.

True healing is not necessarily a cure, but a completion of God's work in body, mind, emotions and spirits.

Death sometimes leads us to question things we had taken for granted before. Does God really exist? Does He love me? How could He let this happen?

God welcomes honest searching. Islam is based on historical fact, not on the speculations of human beings with their limited intellects. Truth stands our clear from error (2:256), it will not collapse under investigation. Ask your questions, seek your answers. Ask for the wisdom that will lead you to Him. Search the Qur'an for answers—find out for yourself what it says about the things you are questioning. After having experienced suffering or the grief-pangs of bereavement for yourself you may find yourself coming to a new level of commitment, one that is perhaps truly meaningful for the first time.

But you will have some questions that cannot be answered, because God chooses not to tell us everything. Many, many things will remain a mystery in this world.

Abdullah ibn Mas'ud was once walking with the Prophet 鑿 when some Jews asked him about the soul. The Prophet 鑿 stood silent and gave no reply, and Abdullah realised that he was being given a revelation, so he stood quietly beside him. The revelation given was: 'They ask you about the soul. Say: 'The soul is by the commandment of my Lord, and of knowledge you are given only a little.' (17:58, Muslim 6712).

God has given us enough information so that the most intellectual person can be satisfied, yet He leaves enough out so that we must all have faith without fully understanding.

Don't worry; instead, pray, and tell God your needs, and don't forget to thank Him for His answers and His blessings. If you do this you will experience God's peace, which is far more wonderful than the human mind can understand.

Don't waste your time with cries of 'if only.' Regret is a wasted emotion; it is futile, for we cannot go back and change things around. No amount of self-recrimination can change the past. Of course you have made mistakes—we all do that, and some of these mistakes have heavy consequences. Don't waste you life in remorse. As long as you did the best you could at the time, that is as much as is expected of you.

Don't be pre-occupied with regret. If you did or said something wrong, confess it to God, and accept His forgiveness. Bring the entire situation before Him, commit it to Him, and leave it there.

True believers have nothing to fear in the most gloomy scenes of life; they have nothing to fear in the valley of death; they have nothing to fear in the grave; they have nothing to fear in the world beyond. For God is with them. They do not go anywhere alone—for God is the Companion, the Guide.

Dying people seem to enter the final valley alone. The friends accompany as far as they can, and then they must give the parting hand. They can cheer the dying ones until they are deaf to all their sounds; they can cheer them with their looks until their eyes become dim and they can see no more; they can cheer them with a fond embrace until they become insensible to every expression of earthly affection, and then they seem to be alone. But dying believers are not alone. God is with them in that valley, and will never leave them. On His promise they can depend, and by that

Presence they can be comforted, until they emerge from the gloom into the bright world beyond. All that is needed to dissipate the terrors of that valley is to be able to say 'You are with me, O Lord.'

Chapter 11

What will happen to me after I die?

Every soul shall have a taste of death; and only on the Day of Judgement shall you be paid your full recompense (3:185; 29:57).

All people have to die. There is little one can do about this to console non-believers who, with no concept of the reality of the soul, are naturally distressed to think that their existence is over and they will cease to be. Believers take a different and more interesting point of view. They are confident that their souls can exist quite independently from their bodies, and will sooner or later leave their bodies and continue to live as individual entities, even though their corpses will rot away and their atoms go back to replenish the soil from which they were made.

What happens to people's souls during the time between the placing of a person's body in the grave and the Account on the Day of Judgement is one of the mysteries of *al-Ghayb* (the unknown) for which there are numerous theories but no scientific proof. Muslims have no doubts that they go on existing, but whether they are 'at rest' or are highly active is a matter about which we can say 'God knows best.'

First and foremost, Allah, speaking through the Qur'an, encourages people not to fear death but to accept it with patience and resignation as an inevitable part of our life process, and to keep in our minds the happy notion that 'death' is not the end of existence. It is not. Furthermore, He assures us that there is no need to react with grief and regret like atheists do (i.e. people who have no belief in God or the Afterlife); the 'dead' are still very much alive!

> 'O believers! Don't be like the unbelievers, who say of their (dead friends): 'If only they had stayed with us they would not have died, or been killed.' ..Don't think of those who are slain in God's way as dead. No, they are alive, finding their sustenance in the Presence of their Lord; they are rejoicing in the bounty provided by God; and with regard to those left behind, who have not yet joined them, (i.e. the believing mourners), the ('dead') glory in the fact that on them is no fear, nor have they (cause to) grieve. They glory in the grace and bounty from God, and in the fact that God does not suffer the reward of the faithful to be lost.' (3:156, 169-171)

In recent years there has been a very interesting development of an aspect of dying which has been known by hearsay for centuries, but which has only recently been made commonplace by the dramatic advances of medical science. People who have been at the bedsides of the dying have always reported what was said, seen or experienced by their patients or loved ones as they approached death. Sometimes, for example, the dying who had been unconscious, or with minds 'wandering' and not aware of the people in the room, have regained temporary consciousness, and revealed changes in their awareness which make those observers feel they have indeed come back from beyond the threshold of death.

These instances refer to what is generally known as 'Near Death Experiences.' Sceptics are correct in pointing out that this cannot give us scientific or factual evidence about the state of death itself, since the individuals concerned had not actually died. Nevertheless, even before the moment of death—while still capable of conversing sensibly with living observers—they have undergone exhilerating experiences, sometimes totally unexpected, which have caused a drastic change in their mood and outlook.

They maybe saw someone, or felt they were leaving the body and entering a new realm, which cheered them up considerably. I have myself had two experiences of this nature, once when I was near death from a serious illness, and once when I was involved in a road accident.

The most interesting of these reports involve a dying person suddenly seeing another person (unseen by the bedside watchers) who was himself or herself dead at the time, but this was not known to the dying one.

These experiences are highly fascinating, but nowadays there is yet another aspect to reporting of death-bed experiences; we now have a mass of information about the experiences of those who have actually been deemed to have *passed* the moment of death, and had been *classified as dead*.

The threshold of death, of course, is notoriously difficult to define. In the old days it was enough that the heart stopped beating and the lungs stopped breathing. These days, the addition of scientific equipment such as the electro-encephalograph records death in other ways—for example, the wavy line becomes a continuous flat line.

It is now a commonplace fact that many people who actually were counted as dead suddenly came back after that moment of passing, restored by medical science—for example, recipients of immediate post-death electric shock treatment, heart massage, or the 'kiss of life.' To the amazement of sceptics and atheists, it is quite clear from these medical findings that dying patients continue to have a conscious awareness of their environment even after being pronounced clinically dead! How can we possibly know this? Simply because nowadays, thanks to these improvements in health care and various processes which can be used to 'bring back' a person after their actual moment of death, the patients themselves can speak up and report back what they saw, felt and heard as they passed beyond the moment of death.

This higher success-rate of resuscitation of those who had been declared clinically dead has resulted in literally thousands of studies of individual accounts of what it actually felt like, and what was seen, heard and experienced. When we compare these cases with the revelation in 3:156-171, we find some very interesting details that support the clear statement that the 'dead' are still 'alive.'

The cases present an enormous range of experiences and phenomena, certain details of which crop up again and again, no matter what the racial or religious background of the 'dead' person; however, it does appear that the more religious the person, the more their experiences can be given a religious interpretation (and these vary slightly according to the faith of the 'deceased').

Many report the experience, immediately before the moment of death, of floating out of their physical bodies and viewing the scene of the deathbed from some other vantage point, frequently close to the ceiling, or even just above it, or somewhere else in the room. Many become aware of other beings, sometimes loved ones who have died before them, and very frequently of an 'angelic' being, 'a being of light,' who is not a human but seems to have been sent as a guide from God. (This is completely in keeping with Muslim teaching.)

Others experience exquisite sweet odours, and feel themselves passing through either a dark tunnel with a bright light at the end of it, or through a very bright tunnel; many experience a panoramic instantaneous 'playback' of the incidents of their lives which is frequently of a judgemental nature in that they are also

brought fully to a realisation of the consequences of
their actions on the people they have affected. They
may then approach some kind of barrier—a lake, mist,
door, fence, window or gate—at which they are met by
some authoritative figure (if they have not already
encountered the 'being of light') and where a decision
is made as to whether or not they are to go back into
the life of the body. The majority of these reports are
happy and exhilarated, but a few are quite the contrary. Those with a lot to feel guilty about find the
experience horrendous and upsetting.

Whatever the experiences, if the individual 'comes
back' to life on earth, he or she is usually totally
changed by the experience.[1]

From my own personal experience, here is a typical example in considerable detail, recounted to me by
a lady friend of mine who 'died' in childbirth. She
suddenly became aware that she was floating just near
the ceiling, and when she turned and looked down,
she saw her own vacated body lying on the bed, and
the nurses dealing with her baby that had just been
born. She knew the sex of the baby, and that it was
perfectly all right. To her consternation, however, the
medical team did not try to resuscitate her, but a nurse
drew the sheet up over her head. This upset her,

---

1. Many cases are reported in such books as 'Life after Life,' R. Moody,
   1976; 'Living with Death and Dying,' E. Kubler-Ross, 1982; 'The After-
   Death Experience,' I. Wilson, 1987; 'Return from Death,' M. Grey, 1985;
   'Testimony of Light' H. Greaves, 1969; 'The Soul's Journey after
   Death,' L. Mabrouk, Dar al-Taqwa, 1987.

because as far as she was concerned she was still alive, but before she had time to think what to do she found herself floating out of the room and along the corridor to the canteen where the night staff were having their cup of tea. There she could not make anybody see or hear her, but she could hear what they were saying. Then she felt sucked back, and fell down with an almighty thump, and sat up (still covered in the sheet) to the amazement of a nurse who was praying quietly by her side. She was able to recount what she saw and heard in the canteen, and when the staff checked, it was found to be quite accurate. She was immensely excited by the experience, and has never forgotten it, and is now no longer afraid to die.

People who have progressed as far as out-of-the-body experience into the realm of what happens after death frequently describe feelings of intense joy, love and peace and fascination, and many do not wish to return to the body. Those who do, however, often return with a thump, and wake up (either with great disappointment or great relief—depending on what they had experienced) to find themselves back with the old pains of their human condition.

All the people who have had such an experience insist that it is nothing like a dream, and indeed, they remember it vividly for the rest of their lives. For many people, the experience is so affecting that the rest of their lives are entirely changed by it.

These facts have to be stated, since these experiences apply to people from all walks of life and are not confined to any particular nation, culture, ethnic group, age range, or to any particular mode of dying. Cross-cultural studies now in progress have proved that they are universal to human beings everywhere.

Muslims, of course, accept without question that all people have souls. The Qur'an indicates that it is perfectly possible for the soul to leave the body even before the moment of death:

> 'It is He who takes your souls by night, and has knowledge of all that you did by day.' (6:60)

> 'Their limbs (souls) do forsake their beds of sleep, while they call upon their Lord in fear and hope.' (32:16)

Many Muslims might well wonder how the reported case studies are relevant to Islam. As it happens, the case studies have revealed nothing that is incompatible with the Quranic teachings and traditions of Islam; in fact, they are rather more compatible with Islam than they are with Christianity or Hinduism, for example. Christians and Hindus who study them are actually obliged to rethink some of their doctrinal conclusions in the light of the evidence—no doubt to the embarrassment of preachers who have presented a traditionally different interpretation of what happens after death. There is no reason to think that those reporting the cases are lying, or have conferred with each other, or been unduly influenced by reading about them or seeing media programmes. They are normal, down-to-earth folks, made serious by their brush with death.

Muslims might perhaps take pride in the fact that as in many other areas of science, the Qur'an once again supports scientific principles rather than mythology.

Muslims would maintain, of course, that it is not really the activities of the medical team that can snatch a person's soul back from death, but Allah's will. One of the most important Quranic ayats on this topic is probably 39:42:

'It is God who takes the souls at death..those on whom He has passed the decree of death He keeps back (from returning to life), but the rest He sends forth (to their bodies) for a term appointed. Truly in this are signs for those who think deeply.'

Those who try to deny the descriptions given by people who have had near-death experiences, and regard them as mere fancy and imagination, should indeed ponder on these words from Allah. Tafsir of the twenty-first century should certainly keep an open mind on the subject, and not try to sweep the experience of so many millions under the carpet.

Obviously, people who do not believe in al-Ghayb, Akhirah, and the existence of souls and angels must necessarily rack their brains for alternative interpretations of what takes place. It does indeed come as a great shock when dying atheists suddenly get the awareness of angels, just the same as believers.

I suppose it needs pointing out that people only enjoy the free will of whether they will believe in Allah, angels and all the rest of it *while they are existing in physical life on earth*. God never forces anyone to believe any of it; it is a matter of their free choice whether they accept or reject belief. However, once they arrive at the conclusion of their earthly lives and enter that realm of al-Ghayb for themselves, that freewill of choice is gone.

Before that ultimate awareness dawns on them, non-believers find the whole notion of the Afterlife, souls and angels as a matter to scoff at, babyish nonsense, wishful thinking for which there is no proof. They regard the comments and experiences of those who are dying as embarrassing lapses of rationality in their loved ones or patients. The usual response is to try not to hear what they say, to silence them, even to drug them. However, the perhaps unexpected awareness of angels or the presence of other souls can bring great comfort not only to the dying, but to the bereaved who are being given signs or clues on to what may happen to them too, in due course. The Prophet ﷺ actively provided information for those who did not have the ability to see what was happening. Here is a specific example.

Jabir ibn 'Abdullah recorded that the dead and mutilated body of his father was brought to him, covered with a cloth. He tried to lift the cloth, but people advised him not to. However, Allah's Messenger ﷺ ordered it to be lifted. He heard the noise of a woman mourner, and asked who it was. They said: 'the daughter (or sister) of 'Amr.' Whereupon he said:

'Why does she weep? The angels are providing him shade with the help of their wings, while he is being lifted (to his heavenly abode).' (Muslim 6041).

The Qur'an frequently mentions these angels. Some passages specifically mention the Angel of Death:

> 'He is the Irresistible, (watching) from above over His worshippers, and He sets guardians over you. At length, when death approaches one of you, Our angels take his soul; and they never fail in their duty.' (6:61)

> 'The Angel of Death, put in charge of you, will take your souls; then shall you be brought back to your Lord.' (32:11).

Here is one reference that mentions a conversation between departed souls and the angelic beings. It brings increased awareness to those 'dead' people—in these cases not an awareness they are pleased to receive:

> 'When the angels take the souls of those who die in sin against their souls, they say: 'What excuse have you (for your behaviour on earth)?' They reply that they (sinned because they) were weak and oppressed on earth. The angels say: 'Was not the earth of God spacious enough for you to move yourselves away from (that) evil?' Such people will find their abode in Hell—what an evil refuge!' (4:97).

The hadiths do not give much information, but they do indicate that the soul of the dying person does not necessarily immediately lose all interest in the body it has vacated, and certainly retains conscious awareness. For example, Muhammad ibn al-Nu'man al-Muqri recorded how a 'dead' friend of his was deeply moved by the simple act of someone gently closing his eyes. He said: 'I heard a man who was devoted to Allah say: 'I closed the eyes of Ja'far al-Muallim when he was dying. He was a man devoted to Allah. On the night (after) he died, I saw him in a dream. He told me: 'The biggest thing for me was your closing of my eyes before I died." (Abu Dawud, 3112).

Although the hadith actually says 'before I died,' it is obvious that as far as his friend was concerned, Ja'far had passed away, and his eyes had fallen into the fixed stare of death. Yet the 'dead' man knew who had helped him and what he had done, and took the trouble to come back in a dream and thank him.

Anas ibn Malik recorded the Prophet's ﷺ statement that when people are placed in the grave, they can hear the footsteps of their mourners as they leave the cemetery: 'When the servant is placed in his grave and his companions retrace their steps, he hears the noise of their footsteps.' (Muslim 6862-3-4; see also Abu Dawud 4733-4-5). He also recorded the soul sitting up and then leaving the body and having experiences, while the corpse was lying tightly bound in its shroud and buried in the grave, unable to move.

'Then two angels come to him and make him sit, and (question him about belief in Allah's Apostle, and show him what would have been his seat in Hell which was exchanged for a seat in Paradise because of his belief.' (Muslim 6862).

The Prophet ﷺ also made it clear by his practice (sunnah) that he believed the souls of the dead were perfectly well able to hear what was being said about them. He frequently used to go to the graveyard of al-Baqi' and sit by the graves of his dead loved ones, and speak to them:

'Umar listened to the words of Allah's Messenger ﷺ and said: 'Allah's Messenger, how can they listen and respond to you? They are dead, and their bodies have decayed.' Thereupon he said: 'By Him in Whose hand is my life, they can hear what I am saying just as distinctly as you, but they lack the power to reply' (Muslim 6869).

There are two passages in the Qur'an that are frequently used by those who reject out-of-body experience or soul experience after death as evidence to prove that the idea of the dead hearing the living is wrong. These passages are:

'You cannot make the dead to hear, nor can you make the deaf to hear the call, when they show their backs and turn away. Nor can you lead back the blind from straying. Only those will you make to hear who believe in Our signs and submit.' (30:52-53).

'The living and those who are dead are not alike. God can make any hear that He wills to hear; but you cannot make those hear (when they) are in (their) graves. You are no more than a warner.' (35:22-23).

At first sight, these verses do seem to be in direct

opposition to the hadiths mentioned above and the Prophet's own frequent practice. If that really is the case, the revelation of the Qur'an must take precedence of the hadith—which must then be false. Much more serious, it must mean that the Prophet ﷺ wasted a great deal of his precious time indulging in personal emotions in graveyards.

However, the meaning of these verses is dependant upon the interpretation of word 'hear'. If you read carefully, you can see that the verb is not being used in the literal sense of ears hearing sound, but in the sense of individuals being converted, being made to accept or be influenced by the words of those who are trying to convert them. It means that after the moment of death has passed, so has a person's opportunity to repent, or benefit from the warnings of believers. 'To hear' in these verses does not mean 'to pick up sounds,' but means 'to listen to the message of God's existence and the complete system of justice, afterlife, etc. and accept it as personal faith. Once they have completed their earthly life and 'death,' their 'books' are completed and sealed ready for the Day of Judgement.

In other words, these verses do not contradict the Prophet's words and practice at all. They are perfectly consistent with it.

So often, well-meaning people without knowledge try to comfort and soothe the bereaved by suggesting to them that death is like 'going to sleep,' or that it is a 'time of forgetting;' they rather ignorantly suggest that when a person dies, all one's woes are forgotten, and all the painful and troubling memories are obliterated. Others think that death is simply the annihilation of all conscious experience altogether. These statements really seem to be the very opposite of what 'dead' people report to be the case!

For a start, the 'dead' person is not alone, but is looked after either by heavenly beings, or loved ones who have already 'died.' They frequently see them at their bedside even before they have 'died.' Muslim studies of the subject have not yet been made, but other studies often report how surprised the dying person is. The last words uttered and reported by their death-bed sitters are usually not inspiring phrases or words of sober import, but shocked gasping out of someone's name, with the obvious attitude that this was not something that had been expected. Some editors have made collections of noble last words, and some people might actually ponder in advance what these famous last words are going to be. Muslims might well hope their last words will be the shahadah, or mention of Allah. What no-one really expects is the equivalent of : Why, James Smith (Abdul Karim)— what are *you* doing here?'

Umar ibn 'Abdul 'Aziz was a devout Muslim, well composed and mentally alert on his death-bed. He wanted and intended to die asking Allah's forgiveness for his sins.

'Ibn Abid-Dunya mentions that on the day 'Umar ibn 'Abdul-'Aziz died, he asked his friends to sit with him. They heard him say: 'I am the one You commanded, and I failed you. You forbade me, and I rebelled.' He said this three times, then he said: 'There is no God but Allah.' (So far, so good. Then the unexpected happened and his last words were not as intended.) He (suddenly) raised his head and stared. They said: 'You are staring (at something) very intently, Amir al-Mu'minin.' He replied: 'I see a presence which is neither man nor jinn.' Then he died.' (reference after next quote.)

Muhammad ibn Wasi was more specific in his report of what he saw: 'Fadala ibn Dinar was with Muhammad ibn Wasi when he died, and heard him say: 'Welcome to my Lord's angels.'[1]

Obviously, the expectations of the dying person towards the Afterlife will vary considerably according to what they have believed and how they have lived. Some don't believe in Afterlife at all, and try desperately to cling on to their earthly bodies; some are happy and expectant and others are apprehensive:

> 'Nay, but you love this fleeting life, and leave alone the Hereafter! Some faces that day will beam, looking towards their Lord, and some faces will be dismal and sad, in the thought that some back-breaking calamity is about to be inflicted on them.' (Yet, whatever their attitude, it cannot prevent their taste of death when their time comes). 'Yes, when (the with-

---

1. Recorded by Ibn al-Qayyim in 'The Soul's Journey after death,' L. Mabrouk, Dar al-Taqwa, 1987, p. 5.

drawing soul) is reaching the collar-bone (as the person nears the moment of death), there will be a cry: 'Who is a magician (to restore him)?' And the dying person will know that this is the time (of parting), and one leg will be joined with another (for burial). That day the drive will be to your Lord.' (75:20-30).

When my own grandmother died, I saw at her bedside a presence I can only assume was the soul of her own mother—for when she finally did die and my father was sitting by her, in the very chair where I had seen the shadowy lady, she turned and stared at him with great joy and her last words were not to him, but to the person she (and I) saw: 'Can I come now, Mum?'

Abu Hurayrah reported what the Prophet ﷺ said about the joyful reunion of the soul of the person who has just died with loved ones who have gone before—a joy that is full of wonder and emotion:

'When a believer is about to die, the angels come with a white sheet of silk and say, 'Come out, good soul, well pleased and well pleasing, to a world of mercy and roses, and to meet a Lord who is not displeased.' It comes out with an odour which is more pleasing than musk. The angels hand him over one to the other until they get him to the Gate of Heaven, where its angels say: 'What a pleasant odour has come with you from earth!' They bring him over to meet the spirits of believers who are more joyful to meet him than anyone of you when he meets a dear relative who has come back after a long absence.' (An-Nisa'i)

In the UK, we have recently celebrated the 50th anniversary of the end of World War II. I was deeply moved by the love still shown for long-dead family and comrades by the survivors, some very ancient survivors whose memories stretched back to World War I! The media was full of memories and sentiments. Yet it occurred to me how wonderful it would be if the saddened survivors could only see things from the 'other side.' Most of these aged folk will die themselves in the next year or two. Just imagine their wonderful joy when they suddenly discover that the loved one they had remembered and grieved for all those years had known all along of their constant love, and appreciated it. Think of what a reunion it will be, how blessed, how amazing and happy. For many 'old soldiers' who have been left behind by friends and family though reason of their old age, the moments after death —insha' Allah—will turn out to be the happiest of their lives!

> 'One day He will gather them together; it will
> be as if they had waited for no more than an
> hour of a day; they will recognize each other.'
> (10:45)

However, the joy is not for all. Not every newly-dead person finds the experience enjoyable. It depends how they have lived, what sort of soul they are. The fate of those people who have deliberately insisted on doing evil and have totally rejected God will not find death a pleasant prospect. Indeed, such people generally resist dying with all their might. They have no wish to face what will come. Their souls do not rise gently and with peaceful acceptance and joy, but have to be taken by force.

> 'By the angels who tear out (the souls of the wicked) with violence; by those who gently draw out (the souls of the blessed).' (79:1-2)

> 'And the stupor of death will bring the truth (before his or her eyes): 'This was the thing you were trying to escape!'..and there will come forth every soul. With each soul will be an angel to drive and an angel to bear witness.' (50:19-21)

Abu Hurayrah recorded a long hadith suggesting the different fates for the good and evil souls:

'When the soul of a believer goes out (of its body) it is received by two angels who take it to the 'sky.' Hammad (one of the narrators) mentioned the sweetness of its odour, (and further said) that the dwellers of the 'sky' say: 'Here comes a pious soul from the realm of the earth. Let there be blessings of Allah upon the body in which it resides. And it is carried (by the angels) to its Lord, the Exalted and Glorious. He will say: 'Take it to its destined end.' And if the person is a nonbeliever, as it (the soul) leaves the body—(Hammad made a mention of its foul smell and of its being cursed)—the dwellers of the 'sky' say: 'Here comes a dirty soul from the realm of earth. Take it to its destined end.' Abu Hurayrah further recorded that Allah's Messenger ﷺ covered his nose with a thin cloth which he had on him while making mention (of the foul smell) of the soul of a nonbeliever.' (Muslim 6867)

Quranic descriptions are numerous and graphic:

> 'If you could but see how the wicked (fare) in
> the flood of confusion at death! The angels
> reach out their hands (for them) saying: 'Yield
> up your souls! This day you shall receive your
> reward—a penalty of shame, because you
> used to tell lies against God and scornfully
> reject His signs.' (6:93)

> 'Those who reject faith and die rejecting—on
> them is God's curse, and the curse of angels
> and of all mankind.' (2:161)

> 'The eyes will fixedly stare in horror—they
> run forward with necks outstretched, their
> heads uplifted, their gaze returning not to-
> ward them, and their hearts a gaping void.'
> (14:42-43)

Aghast at what will happen to them, a fate they had so foolishly and arrogantly sneered at and denied, they try all sorts of tricks and excuses, but to no avail. None can help them now, and they are doomed to their penalty, if God wills.

Such is the sad conclusion of their lives.

> 'Every soul that has sinned, if it possessed
> everything on earth, would willingly give it
> in ransom. When they see the Penalty they
> declare how sorry they are; but the judgement
> on them is with justice.' (10:54).

The exact details of the relationship between the soul and the mortal remains of each individual, until the Time of Judgement, is part of al-ghayb, the unknown. Muslim teaching suggests that souls of the good and evil will either enjoy or really hate the waiting time, the state known as Barzakh. The human remains, of course, meet different fates—they either moulder away or are eaten by worms in the grave, or perhaps are cremated or lost at sea, and so on. Even so, Muslim tradition suggests that they are aware of some sort of experience, the good souls wandering far and wide while still connected to their mortal remains, and the wicked souls crushed and confined and tormented.

Al-Bara ibn Azib recorded that 'a space will be made (in the grave of the good soul) as far as the eye can see, whereas the grave of the evil soul will be restricted so that his ribs will be pressed together.' (Abu Dawud 4735)

It is a fearful matter to ponder. We wonder what are our own chances when our own times come? Everyone has sinned, of course—there is no such thing as a person who has lived totally without falling short in some way. This realisation might make some dying people highly anxious over any impending punishment or doom for their sins. It is important to realise that God's judgement and punishment is for the deliberate and hardened sinners who have not repented. Those of us who are just ordinary weak believers who have done numerous wrong things, but who are genuinely sorry, are forgiven, insha' Allah. This is stressed in the Qur'an over and over again by our Lord, the Compassionate One, and in numerous hadiths of the Blessed Prophet:

'Those who believe and work righteous deeds—from them shall We blot out all evil in them, and We shall reward them according to the best of their deeds.' (29:7).

> 'God will turn off from them the worst in their deeds, and give them the reward according to the best of what they have done.' (39:35)

> 'If anyone does good, the reward is better than the deed; but if anyone does evil, they are only punished (to the extent) of their deeds.' (28:84)

> '(To the righteous soul will be said): O soul, in rest and satisfaction come back to your Lord—well pleased, and well pleasing to Him.' (89:27-28).

When Abdul 'Aziz ibn Sulayman died, he and his friends had apparently been concerned about whether they would be forgiven for their sins. Abdul 'Aziz appeared to one of these friends, in a dream and reassured him on this point. The friend asked him what death had felt like, and what his present experiences were like. He replied: 'Do not ask (or worry) about the intensity of grief and sorrow of death! Allah's mercy concealed all our faults and we encountered nothing but His bounty.'[1]

Non-believers have mocked the notion of life beyond death since the beginning of time. Surah 75 reassures us:

---

1. From 'The Soul's Journey after death,' L. Mabrouk, Dar al-Taqwa, 1987, p. 30.

> 'Do people think We cannot (resurrect them and) bring their bones back together again? Truly, we are able to restore even their fingerprints.' (75:3-4).

To create us anew is no more difficult for Allah than to create us the first time. The quoted verse is so significant, of course, because at the time of the Prophet ﷺ humans had not discovered the unique individual and identifying properties of finger prints—a discovery that waited until the end of the nineteenth century![1]

So let us not ignore people's experiences as they face and enter 'death.'

Paying attention to dying people's observations are of tremendous importance to the successful dealing with the mourning process of those left behind. It may well change the entire attitude of the bereaved towards their own future deaths. If they can realise that the souls of the vast majority are released from their suffering bodies even before that body draws its last breath, and that they painlessly and with great joy enter a new and active state, then death for believers has truly lost its sting.

1. I have drawn attention to this scientific fact, unknown to humans in the century when the Qur'an was revealed, in my small booklet 'Fingerprints' Ta-Ha Publishers Ltd., 1992.

Chapter 12

Islamic Burial

ISLAMIC BURIAL

In some countries, Muslims find themselves obliged to conform to local practices which are different from the precepts of Islam, especially on the subject of the laying out and burial of the dead. This is sometimes due to the lack of Muslim facilities, and sometimes due to the ignorance of some Muslims of the correct procedure. The following chapter presents all the points on which all four orthodox schools of Islamic law agree.

Every Muslim hopes that when their time comes, they will die peacefully in Muslim surroundings, attended by Muslim people who understand the sensitivities and religious requirements of Islam. However, sometimes Muslims may die in hospital where the staff may not be aware of Muslim needs, or may be indifferent to them. They may not wish to allow Muslims to take the deceased's body and wash it themselves. Cemeteries may not have special facilities for Muslims; if the cemetery is laid out according to a garden scheme, or according to Christian or Jewish faiths, it may not be possible for the deceased to be buried facing Makkah. In some places, it may be difficult to find space for only one Muslim to be buried in each grave.

When Muslims face conditions over which they have no control, they are not held at fault by Allah when they accept what is available; however, it is commendable to try to fulfil all the conditions laid out here, if possible.

DUTIES WHEN A LOVED ONE IS DYING

People who are born Muslims should be welcomed into the world by the purification of their bodies and by joyful exclamations of 'There is no God but Allah!' They hope to be bidden farewell at death by the ritual washing, the shrouding of their body by loved ones, and by prayer said over them.

When Muslims are at the point of death, they should if possible be turned so that they are facing in the direction of Makkah. This can be done in several ways; the best is to place them on their right side, with their faces turned towards the Ka'bah. The second way is to lie them on their backs, with their feet in the direction of the Ka'bah, and their heads raised slightly so that their faces are turned towards the qiblah. If the dying person is in a movable bed, it is often quite a simple matter to turn the bed to the correct position without disturbing the occupant overmuch.

The dying one should then be encouraged to think about Allah by somebody saying aloud so that they can hear—'There is no God but Allah, and Muhammad ﷺ is the Prophet of God.'

'Abu Sa'id al-Khudri recorded: 'Encourage the recitation of 'There is no God but Allah' to those of you who are dying.' (Muslim 1996, Abu Dawud 3111).

Mu'adh ibn Jabal recorded the Apostle of Allah ﷺ as saying: 'If anyone's last words are 'There is no God but Allah,' he will enter Paradise.' (Abu Dawud 3110). (This in no way implies that those who do *not* say it will not go to Paradise. It simply means that those who die in belief will, insha' Allah).

This should not be done insensitively, however, in case the dying person is disquieted. Usually the dying person is very well aware that these are the final moments, and they are usually reconciled to it and prepared to 'slip away.' It is not the right of an observer, however well-meaning, to force this aware-ness on to somebody and give the impression of 'hurrying them along.' That would be highly tactless.

It is the *ideal* in Islam if the dying words of a person can be the life-long affirmation of their faith, but this is not a matter for fanaticism. If he or she can say the 'kalimah,' well and good. A person attending the death bed may encourage them to say it, but they should not insist in case the dying one is in pain, or not in full control of his or her powers. Tactless insistence might lead the person to say something unbecoming instead. If the dying person is unable to speak, the words may be thought mentally. God is not disap-pointed if these are *not* their last words; He knows best. He understands very well the state of the dying person's heart and beliefs. It is far more important that

the dying person dies in the *state of belief* of those
words, than that they actually are made to mutter
them. Any well-meaning Muslims who made their
piety a matter of distress to a dying person would be
going against the spirit of Islam, and would not be
appreciated.

It is always preferable if someone of the dying
person's nearest and dearest family or friends, one
who will be the gentlest helper, should be at their side
to help them turn their thoughts to God the Most High,
so that they may feel at peace, and so that they may
anticipate the loving grace of their Lord, and also to
remind them gently to repent of their sins and make
their last requests and farewells. The dying need not
fear that all their thoughts and love of God will be
proved wrong by discovering in the end that Allah is
totally different from what they have thought.

'I am as My servant expects to find Me.'

Many prayers for the dying and for those who will
be bereaved by their parting should be offered up, and
passages from the Qur'an, especially surah Yasin
(Surah 36—'Surely We shall give life to the dead' etc.)
should be recited—though the reciter must recite inau-
dibly so as not to disturb the dying person. Once again,
it is unkind and unnecessary to make a dying person
feel as if they are being hurried into the next world, and
perhaps even being made to feel they are being a
nuisance if they linger on.

As soon as the person has died, all recitation in

their presence may stop. Some people think continued recitation is preferable, if not obligatory. It is not obligatory—it is not even sunnah, and the early Muslims did not continue to recite. If a relative or loved one feels that they wish to go on reciting, that is a matter for them—but it is not sunnah. The eyes should be gently closed, and the body covered.

The moving death of the Blessed Prophet's ﷺ friend Abu Salamah is recorded in the hadith, with a good example of a farewell prayer:

Umm Salamah—who later married the Blessed Prophet ﷺ—recorded: The Messenger of Allah ﷺ came to Abu Salamah. (He died with) his eyes fixed open. He (the Prophet ﷺ) closed them, and then said: 'When the soul is taken away, the sight follows it.' Some of the people of Abu Salamah's family wept and wailed, so he said: 'Do not entreat for yourselves anything other than good, for the angels will say 'Amen' to what you say.' He then said: 'O Allah, forgive Abu Salamah, raise him to high rank among those who are rightly-guided; make him as a guardian of his descendants who survive him. Forgive us and him, O Lord of the Universe, and make his grave spacious and grant him light in it.' (Muslim 2003).

DUTIES AFTER DEATH AND BEFORE WASHING

Although Muslims believe that the soul has departed at the moment of death, and that which is left behind is nothing but an empty shell—nevertheless the mortal remains of a Muslim should be treated with dignity, love and respect, and the last services done to them in a prayerful and loving atmosphere.

What should be done after death before they are washed? Firstly, to preserve dignity, their eyes should be closed and a cloth tied round their lower jaw to bind it up, so that the mouth does not sag open in an ugly and undignified manner.

Abu Dawud reported that he heard Muhammad ibn al-Nu'man tell that he heard a man who was devoted to Allah say: 'I closed the eyes of Ja'far al-Mu'allim when he was dying. He was a man devoted to Allah. I saw him in a dream on the night he died. He said: 'The greatest thing you did for me was the closing of my eyes before I died.' (Abu Dawud 3112).

Something suitable should be placed over the abdomen so that it does not become inflated. A heavy plate, or a hot-water-bottle filled with cold water, both wrapped in a cloth, are suitable examples.

Straight after death the deceased's joints should be loosened up, if this is possible. If it is not possible, it is not something that should be forced. The loosening is done as follows—the forearms are flexed back to the upper arms, the upper arms to the sides of the body; likewise the lower legs are flexed to the thighs and the thighs to the abdomen. This is not compulsory, but is done to facilitate the washing and shrouding by preventing the body from stiffening.

The deceased should be raised slightly, and turned to face the Ka'bah. They should be undressed and covered with a sheet which conceals the whole of the body. Haste must be made to pay any of their debts that remain outstanding, from the deceased's own property. If the deceased is insolvent, it may be possible to call upon the *zakah* funds of the local Muslim community.

WASHING THE DEAD

This is not just a matter of hygiene or convenience. It is a religious duty, and the performing of it is a collective obligation. In other words, if there is no relative or friend available, the obligation falls upon any member of the community, to see it done as decently as possible.

The person who washes the body of a dead Muslim should himself or herself be an adult Muslim, in full possession of their senses. They should be persons who are honest, trustworthy, and well acquainted with the procedure for Muslim washing of the dead so that they can carry it out in accordance with the sunnah.

They should first mentally form the resolve of carrying out the washing of the deceased. In doing the wash, they should not make public any of the deceased's imperfections in this most private and intimate of moments, drawing attention to them, but should conceal any shortcomings they observe.

The fittest person to wash and shroud a deceased male is whoever the deceased chose himself, then, in order of preference, his father, grandfather, or closest male relative on his side, then on his mother's side. It is also permissible for his wife to wash him.

Aishah recorded: 'By Allah, we did not know whether to take off the clothes of the Apostle of Allah ﷺ as we took off the clothes of our (ordinary) dead, or whether we should wash him while his clothes were on him. When the people differed among themselves, Allah cast slumber over them until everyone of them had put his chin on his chest (i.e. gone to sleep). Then a speaker spoke from a side of the house, and they did not know who he was: 'Wash the Prophet ﷺ while his clothes are on him.' So they stood to the Apostle of Allah ﷺ and washed him while he had his shirt on him. They poured water on his shirt, and rubbed him with his shirt and not with their hands.' Aishah used to say: 'If I had known beforehand about my affair what I have come to know later, none would have washed him except his wives.' (Abu Dawud 3135).

It is the view of the majority of scholars that it is perfectly permissible for spouses to see to the washing of each other.

The Blessed Prophet ﷺ said to Aishah: 'It would not harm you if you should die before me; I should wash you, shroud you, offer prayer over you and bury you.' (Ibn Majah).

This indicates that a husband can wash his wife. It is known that Ali washed the Prophet's ﷺ daughter Fatimah after her death. According to the school of Abu Hanifah, a wife can wash her husband, but a husband may not wash his wife, but this does not appear to be sunnah. Certainly the Prophet's ﷺ wife Aishah was very disappointed that she had not been able to wash her beloved husband herself.

The fittest person to wash a woman is first her mother, then her grandmother, then her closest female relative. It is also permissible for the husband to wash his dead wife, as we have seen.

If the deceased is a young boy, he may be washed by women, and vice versa. If a woman dies, and only men are present none of whom is her husband, then one of these must cleanse her, covering his hand so as not to touch her naked body. Similarly, if a man dies among women none of whom is his wife, a woman may cleanse him using a covering over her hand.

Clean water should be used, and if this cannot be found, the deceased may not be washed. Islam recommends that a body may be cleansed with sand instead, but sand may not be available. Muslims are not obliged to wash unbelievers, an aborted foetus, a dead body where most of the body has been removed (by bomb blast, for example), or those slain in battle. Muslims believe that people who die as martyrs for God in battle should be buried 'with their blood.' Their weapons, belts and everything except their clothes are removed, and they are then buried in the clothes in which they were slain. It is not wrong to shroud them without their clothes, but it is better if the clothes are not removed.

No funeral prayer is performed over the body of someone slain in battle; they are buried without prayer, just as it was commended by the Prophet ﷺ.

Jabir ibn Abdullah recorded: 'On the day of the

Battle of Uhud, my father was brought, and he had been mutilated; he was placed in front of Allah's Messenger ﷺ and a sheet was over him. I went, intending to uncover my father, but my people prevented me. Again I tried to uncover him, but my people forbade me. Allah's Messenger ﷺ gave his order, and he was borne away. At that time he heard the voice of a woman crying, and asked: 'Who is that?' They said: 'It is the daughter of the sister of Amr.' He said: 'Don't weep, for the angels have been shading him with their wings while he was carried away.' (Bukhari 22.33.381).

Jabir recorded: 'A man had an arrow shot in his chest or throat, so he died. He was shrouded in his clothes just as he was.' (Abu Dawud 3127).

Ibn Abbas recorded: 'The Messenger ﷺ commanded to remove weapons and waterskins from the martyrs of Uhud, and that they should be buried with their blood and their clothes.' (Abu Dawud 3128).

Anas ibn Malik recorded: 'The Apostle ﷺ passed Hamzah who was killed and mutilated. He said: 'If Safiyyah had not been grieved, I could have left him until the birds and beasts of prey had eaten him, and he would (still) have been resurrected, from their bellies.' The garments were scanty and the slain were in great number. So one, two and three persons were shrouded in one garment.' (Abu Dawud 3130)

If a pilgrim dies in a state of ritual consecration (in ihram), they should be washed with water, but nothing sweet-smelling should be brought near them, nor should their heads be covered (for a man) or their faces veiled (for a woman), since on the Day of Resurrection they will rise up as pilgrims.

HOW IS THE WASHING DONE?

When it is begun, the deceased should be covered from navel to knee. They must be washed in a secluded, private place.

The washer winds a cloth round the hand, and with this cleans away any impurities from the body of the deceased. (Several cloths and a 'disposal bucket' should be at hand in case there are any severe impurities to be cleansed).

Then the rest of the body is washed with a cloth, and the abdomen pressed lightly, except when the deceased is a pregnant woman, to expel any remaining matter. It is recommended to have incense or other sweet-smelling substance at hand, so that no offensive smell should be perceptible.

First, the head of the deceased should be raised slightly, so that the water from the wash flows down and does not run back towards the head.

Then the washer should insert two fingers wetted with water between the deceased's lips, and clean the teeth, then insert them just into the nostrils and clean them. Then the ritual ablutions should be performed on the deceased just as they were for prayer, except that the water should not enter the deceased's mouth or nose.

The deceased's hair and beard should be washed.

Then water is poured on the body, and first the right side is washed back and front, and then the left side is washed in the same way—with pure water, or water and powdered lotus-leaves, or with any substance which cleanses the body, such as soap. A sweet-smelling substance, like camphor, can be put in the final washing water.

Out of respect for the deceased, the washer should always be gentle in handling the body, and in rubbing the limbs, pressing the abdomen, loosening up the joints, and everything else.

Washing the deceased once all over is a religious duty. However, the sunnah prescribes the repetition of the washing an odd number of times.

If any impurity is discharged from the body after it has been washed, it must be removed and the body rewashed an odd number of times, up to five or seven. However, if the impurity is discharged after the body has been placed in the shroud, the washing is not repeated, but the impurity is removed.

The body should then be dried with a cloth, the hair and beard scented with any substance except saffron, and those parts of the body on which one rests during prostration in prayer also scented—forehead, nose, hands, knees and feet. Likewise, scent is placed on the ears and in the armpits. It is preferable that the scent be camphor.

Umm Atiyya recorded that the Apostle of Allah ﷺ came to us when we were bathing his daughter (Zaynab), and he told us: 'Wash her with water and (with the leaves of) the lote tree, three or five times, or more than that if you think fit; and put camphor or something like camphor in the last washing; then inform me when you have finished.' So when we had finished we informed him, and he gave to us his own wrapping-cloth saying: 'Put this next to her body.' (Muslim 2041). She further said: 'We braided her hair in three plaits, two on the side of her head and one on her forehead.' (Muslim 2047). She also recorded that when the Messenger of Allah ﷺ asked her to wash his daughter, he told her to start from the right side, and with those parts of the body over which wudu is performed.' (Muslim 2048—see also Abu Dawud 3136 for the same washing, and Bukhari 23.9.345).

SHROUDING

The shrouding of a dead Muslim is a collective obligation, except for martyrs slain in battle. The expenses for the deceased's shrouding, preparation for burial and burial should be paid out of that part of the deceased's private assets on which nobody has any claim. If there are no such assets, the shroud should be provided by whoever supported that person when he or she was alive; if they cannot afford it, by the Muslim public treasury, and failing that, by those Muslims who can afford it.

It is not commendable for it to be an expensive piece of material.

Ali ibn Abi Talib recorded: 'Do not be extravagant in shrouding, for I heard the Apostle of Allah ﷺ say: 'It will quickly be decayed.' (Abu Dawud 3148).

A man's preferred shroud should be three white winding sheets, none of them being a shift or turban. The shrouding could, however, be two sheets, or even one, provided it covers the whole of the body. A child may always be shrouded in one sheet, even though there is no objection if relatives wish to provide three.

Aishah recorded that the Messenger of Allah ﷺ was shrouded in three garments of white Yamani stuff from Sahul, among which was neither a shirt nor a turban; and so far as hullah is concerned, there was some doubt about it in the minds of the people, that it was brought for him in order to shroud him with it but it was abandoned, and he was shrouded in three cotton garments of white Yamani stuff from Sahul. Then Abdullah ibn Abu Bakr got it and said: 'I would like to keep this in order to be shrouded myself in it.' He then said: 'If Allah, the Exalted and Majestic, would have desired it for His Apostle ﷺ, he would have been shrouded with it.' So he sold it, and gave its price in charity.' (Muslim 2052).

Hullah is robing consisting of one wrapper for the entire body, tied with a waist wrapper. Abdullah, although sorely tempted because he would dearly have liked to have taken the Prophet's ﷺ shroud for his own use, exerted his high Islamic principles. He did not deem it proper either to use that for his own coffin which the Prophet ﷺ could not use, and he did not even keep it with him as a memento but sold it and distributed its yield among the poor.

First, the shrouds are spread out one on top of the other, and perfumed with incense. The final winding-sheet should be the longest and widest.

The deceased, covered with a sheet, is lifted and laid out on top of the shrouds and perfumed with incense. Then the edge of the top winding-sheet is folded over the deceased's right side, then the other edge over his left side. The second and third sheets are treated in the same way. These are all fastened in place round the deceased, and unfastened only when he is placed in the grave.

If no sheet can be found big enough to cover the entire body, (in primitive circumstances), then the head should be covered with it, and grass or paper placed over the legs. If nothing except what suffices to cover the deceased's private parts is available, then these alone are covered.

Khabbab recorded: Mus'ab ibn Umayr was killed on the Day of Uhud. He had only a striped cloak. When we covered his head with it, his feet stuck out; and when we covered his feet, his head appeared. There-upon the Apostle of Allah ﷺ said: 'Cover his head with it, and cover his feet with some grass.' (Abu Dawud 3149, Bukhari 23.26.365).

If the slain are many, and there are not enough shrouds, then two or three may be shrouded in one winding-sheet and buried in one grave, as was done with the martyrs slain in Uhud, may God be pleased with all of them.

A woman is preferably shrouded in five garments

which are a shift, a waist-wrapper, a winding-sheet, a head-veil and a loin cloth to bind her upper legs. If these are not available, she must be shrouded in whatever suffices to cover her body, as for the man.

Layla bint Qaif al-Thaqafiyyah recorded: 'I was one of those who washed Umm Kulthum, the daughter of the Prophet ﷺ, when she died. The Apostle of Allah ﷺ first gave us a lower garment, then a shirt, then head-wear, then a cloak (which covered the whole body), and then she was shrouded in another garment.' She said: 'The Apostle of Allah ﷺ was sitting at the door and he had the shrouding with him. He passed us the garments one by one.' (Abu Dawud 3151).

First the shrouds are laid out in order, then the deceased lady, covered with a sheet is lifted and laid out on the shrouds and perfumed with incense. The loin-cloth is then bound round her upper legs, and the waist wrapper tied in place. Then she is clothed in the shift. If her hair is long it is plaited into three braids hanging down her back. The head veil is put on her, and she is finally wrapped in the winding-sheet which is fastened in place and unfastened only when she is placed in the grave.

Umm Atiyya recorded of her braiding of the hair of the Prophet's ﷺ daughter Zaynab: 'We braided her hair in three plaits and placed them behind her back, one plait of the front side, and the two side plaits.' (Abu Dawud 3138. This probably does not mean what a western person would mean by three separate plaits, but that the hair was divided into three sections and braided into one three-fold plait, taking one piece straight back from the forehead and gathering the other two pieces from right and left side, and thus forming one plait which lay down the back.)

Hafsah bint Sirin recorded that Umm Atiyya said they had entwined the hair of the daughter of Allah's Messenger ﷺ in three braids. They first undid her hair and washed it, then entwined it in three braids.' (Bukhari 23.14.350).

FUNERAL PRAYER-SALAT AL-JANAZAH

This is a religious duty, and a collective obligation; it has to be performed by at least one Muslim. The fittest person to pray over the deceased is whoever the deceased himself or herself chose prior to their death, provided only that this person is not immoral or a non-believer. After that, in order of preference, the one to give the prayer should be the Imam or his deputy, and deceased's son, grandson or great-grandson; then the closest male relative.

First the resolve (or niyyah) of saying the funeral prayer is expressed from the heart. Then the formula 'God is Most Great' is repeated four times. The first is upon beginning the prayer, and after one recites the Surah al-Fatihah alone, without a following recitation from the Qur'an as is normal. Then the hands are raised while the second takbir is said ('God is Most Great'), and after this the prayer of Ibrahim ﷺ is recited, as follows:

'O Allah, bless Muhammad ﷺ and his family, as you blessed Ibrahim ﷺ and his family. You are the Most Gracious, the Exalted One. Grant Your blessing to Muhammad ﷺ and to his family as You granted it to Ibrahim ﷺ and his family. You are the Most Gracious, the Exalted One.'

Then the hands are raised and the third takbir is said ('Allah is the Most Great'), after which one prays for the deceased, using the traditional prayer as follows:

'O Allah, grant forgiveness to us all, the living and the dead, those present here with us and those absent from us, our young and our old, our men and our women. O Allah, keep those of us who remain here always true to Your will; keep those of us who are experiencing death steadfast in strong faith. O Allah, deprive us not of the recompense for our departed one, and do not subject us to trial as a result of his (or her) death.' (From Abu Dawud 3195, recorded by Abu Hurayrah).

It is also permissible to use prayers other than those quoted here. It is not compulsory to learn these by heart, although many Muslims do. One's own prayers in one's own words are perfectly in order.

Another of the Blessed Prophet's ﷺ beautiful prayers over a dead body was:

O Allah, You are its Lord, You created it, You did guide it into Islam, You have taken its spirit, and You know best its inner nature and outer aspect. We have gathered as intercessors, so forgive him (or her).' (Abu

Dawud 3194—recorded by Abu Hurayrah).

The following prayer could be made here, or at the graveside:

'O Allah, forgive him (or her-throughout), have mercy on him, give him peace and absolve him. Receive him with honour, and make his grave spacious; wash him with water, snow and hail. Cleanse him from faults as You would cleanse a white garment from impurity. Reward him with a home more excellent than his home (was here), with his family (made) more excellent than (it was here), a spouse (made) more excellent than (here). Admit him to the Garden and protect him from the torment of the grave and the torment of the Fire.' (Muslim 2106, recorded by Auf ibn Malik, who said at the end: 'I earnestly desired that I had been that dead body,' because of that prayer.)

Then one raises the hands in the fourth takbir, and here a short silence is kept; or else one may repeat phrases from the above prayer. Then the closing prayer of the salah is said once, and with this the funeral prayer is ended.

Notice that the whole prayer is made standing. There is no prostration or sujud, as in the normal prayer, no bowing and kneeling with foreheads on the earth.

The practice laid down in the sunnah is that the funeral prayer should be performed in a group if a number of Muslims are present, with the Imam or prayer leader standing in front, and those present praying in three rows behind him. If someone comes late, they should join the prayer and when the Imam finishes with the words 'Peace be upon you,' they can then complete their prayer by reciting the sections missed.

The prayer for a child is the same as for an adult, except that after the third takbir, instead of the request for God's forgiveness the following prayer is said:

'O Allah, make him (or her) a runner going on ahead, to lead the way for his (or her) parents, and make him (or her) a recompense and a treasure laid up for them.'

CARRYING THE BIER

The funeral procession should then proceed without delay, for the Blessed Prophet ﷺ said:

'Convey the deceased swiftly, for if he was a good person then you are taking him to good things, and if he was not, then you should lower the evil from your shoulders as quickly as possible.' (Muslim 2061, Bukhari 23.50.401).

People should always stand in respect when a funeral procession passes, even if they do not know who is being buried.

Amir ibn Rabai recorded: 'Should anyone of you come across a funeral procession, even if he does not intend to accompany it, he should stand up until it passes by him or is lowered on the ground.' (Muslim 2091).

The Prophet ﷺ left an example of standing when funerals passed by, even when the deceased was not a member of his own faith.

Jabir ibn Abdullah recorded: 'A bier passed by and the Holy Prophet ﷺ stood up for it, and we also stood up along with him. We said (when we found out): 'Messenger of Allah! That was the bier of a Jewess!' Upon this, he remarked: 'Truly, death is the matter to be concerned about, so whenever you come across a (i.e. any) bier, stand up.' (Muslim 2095; see also Muslim 2098 when the Blessed Prophet stood for a Jewish man, and when questioned said: 'Was he not a human being, and does he not have a soul?')

The Blessed Prophet ﷺ, who lived in a time before the invention of the motor vehicle, always preferred mourners to walk in procession rather than ride.

Thawban recorded: An animal was brought to the Apostle of Allah ﷺ while he was walking with a funeral. He refused to ride on it. When the funeral was over, the animal was brought to him and he rode it. He was asked about it, and said: 'The angels were on their feet. I was not going to ride while they were walking. When they went away, I rode.' (Abu Dawud 3171).

When people are accompanying a funeral procession on foot, they should keep as close to the bier as possible. It does not particularly matter whether they walk in front, behind of, or at the side of the bier.

Al-Mughirah ibn Shubah recorded: 'A rider should go behind the bier and those on foot should walk behind it, in front of it, on its right and on its left, keeping near it.' (Abu Dawud 3174).

Walking to the grave is considered more respectful

than riding, but using vehicles is virtually the universal practice in funerals in the west, especially in crowded cities, or places where the cemetery is a long distance from the place where the deceased is. The principle is to be respectful, without being ostentatious. It is normal these days to hire such things as a black car, or even make use of a funeral company to organise the proceedings. These always behave with respect and dignity, and can be a great consolation to a grieving relative. The vehicle should not speed along at the normal pace, but should proceed gently and slowly.

If there are walkers and vehicles, the walkers should precede the vehicles.

Women were allowed to accompany the procession of mourners, but it was not recommended:

Umm Atiyya recorded: 'We were forbidden to follow the bier, but it was not made absolute on us.' (Muslim 2039).

The way to complete farewells to the deceased attested in the sunnah was to pray and then depart. This can be done in one of three ways:

> praying over the deceased and then leaving;

> following the bier to the grave, then waiting until the deceased has been buried, and then depart:

> Or, those present may wait until the burial, and then pray for God's forgiveness for the deceased and request Him to strengthen him in faith, and pray for mercy for his soul. This is the way most rewarded by Allah.

THE GRAVE

Funerals should be simple and inexpensive. Extravagance is forbidden in Islam, and since there is no class system for the dead, there should be no special cemeteries for the leaders. Mourners should be humble and not ostentatious; they should pay heed to their own end in due course, and take warning from the fact of death and from the fate of the dead.

Mourners at the graveside should not be distracted by people speaking of worldly things or indulging in laughter or idle talk. One would not have thought this appropriate anyway, but sometimes the coming together of friends and relatives, and the atmosphere of release from strain (particularly if the deceased passed away after a long illness, for example) leads to 'small talk' and even high spirits. People at the graveside should remember the sorrow of the bereaved and not behave in a manner that is not appropriate, or that would cause further hurt.

It is recommended that people who are at the graveside should remain standing, and not sit until the deceased has been buried, even if it takes quite a long time; but there is no objection to anyone who arrived early at the graveside before the funeral procession arrived sitting while they wait for it to arrive.

Abu Said al-Khudri recorded: 'Whenever you come across a bier you should stand up, and he who follows it should not sit down until it is placed in the ground.' (Muslim 2094).

The grave should reach the depth of a man's chest,

and should be well made and large. It should be deep enough to prevent any bad smell coming out, to stop animals disturbing the body. The sunnah is that a qiblah niche should be made in the side wall of the grave, as was done in the grave of the Blessed Prophet ﷺ. This niche is a hollow which is dug out at the bottom of the grave in the side of the wall which faces the Ka'bah, and the deceased is placed in it.

'Amir ibn Sa'd ibn Abu Waqqas recorded that Sa'd, during his final illness, said: 'Make a niche for me in the side of the grave, and set up bricks over me, as was done in the case of Allah's Messenger ﷺ.' (Muslim 2112).

The Blessed Prophet ﷺ preferred what was called lahd, a niche in the side of the grave, and then covering it with unbaked bricks. But if the soil was not conducive to this type of lahd, then shiqq, in which the lahd is not prepared in the niche but in the middle of the grave, is also permissible.

If a niche cannot be made, then a trench is dug in the ground for the deceased in the floor of the grave, and after the deceased has been laid in it, it is roofed over so that no earth falls upon the body.

It is preferable if the deceased can be buried in a Muslim cemetery, or a part of a cemetery made over to Muslims, except for martyrs slain in battle, who should be buried where they fall.

It is commendable to put the deceased into the grave from the direction where his feet will be, if that is possible, and it is commendable to cover a woman's grave with a sheet.

A woman should be lowered into her grave by a male relative within the forbidden degrees of marriage. All bodies should be placed in the grave legs first.

Abu Ishaq said that al-Harith left in his will that Abdallah ibn Yazid should offer his funeral prayer, so he prayed over him. He then put him in the grave from the side of his legs, and said: 'This is a sunnah of the Prophet ﷺ.' (Abu Dawud 3205).

The deceased is placed on the right side with the face in the direction of the Ka'bah. He or she should be placed close to the wall, so that they do not fall on their faces, and should be supported by a pile of earth behind them so that they do not roll over on the their backs.

Whoever places them in the grave should say:

'In the name of Allah, we commit you to the earth, according to the way of the Prophet of God ﷺ.'

The fastenings of the shroud at the head and feet are undone. Once the deceased is in place, a wall of bricks is erected next to the body, stopped with mud, to prevent any earth from falling on to it. If there are no bricks, canes or large leaves can be used. Then it is commendable to sprinkle a little dust over the grave three times, saying:

'We created you from it, and return you into it, and from it We will raise you a second time.' (20:55).

After this the earth is heaped over the grave, while people make their own private prayers, or use the beautiful prayers of the Prophet (see p. 26, 143-145).

The surface of the grave should be raised a hand's breadth from the ground (not more than 25-30 cms), so that it will be recognised as a grave and passers-by will take care not to tread upon it, and will pray for God's mercy on the person who is in the grave. It should not be more than that, but the place should be levelled.

Abu'l-Hayyaj as-Asadi recorded that Ali had said to him: 'Should I not send you on the same mission that Allah's Messenger ﷺ sent me? Do not leave an image without obliterating it, or a high grave without levelling it.' (Muslim 2115, Abu Dawud 3212).

It may be marked with a stone, or something to show that it is a grave, but money should not be spent on tombstones or memorials. Instead donations can be given to the poor. The only writing on the grave should be the person's name.

Al-Muttalib recorded that when Uthman ibn Mazun died, he was brought out on his bier and buried. The Prophet ﷺ ordered a man to bring him a stone, but he was unable to carry it; so the Apostle of Allah ﷺ got up and went over to it and rolled up his sleeves. The one who told al-Muttalib remarked: 'I still see the whiteness of the forearms of the Apostle of Allah ﷺ as he rolled up his sleeves.' He then carried it and placed it at his head, saying: 'I am marking my brother's grave with it, and I shall bury beside him those of my family who die.' (Abu Dawud 3200).

Al-Qasim said that he asked Aishah to show him the grave of the Apostle of Allah ﷺ and his two companions. She showed him three graves which were neither high nor low, but were spread with soft red pebbles in an open space. (Abu Dawud 3214).

It is forbidden to make any structure over the grave or to plaster it—this was the pre-Islamic practice. It is also considered wrong and disrespectful to sit on or lean against a grave, and seeking sanctuary among the graves is forbidden.

Jabir recorded that Allah's Messenger ﷺ forbade that the graves should be plastered, or that they be used as sitting places, or that a building should be made over them.' (Muslim 2116, Abu Dawud 3219).

Abu Hurayrah recorded: 'It is better that one of you should sit on live coals which burn his clothing and come in contact with his skin, rather than he should sit on a grave.' (Abu Dawud, 3222).

MAKING GRAVES INTO SHRINES

It is not correct Islam to erect mosques over graves or light lamps over them. The Blessed Prophet ﷺ would have disapproved strongly of the practice carried on in various places in the Muslim world where the resting-places of the faithful have been turned into shrines and tourist attractions. Thinking about these exalted grave-shrines, he said:

'May God curse women who visit the graves, and those who erect mosques and light lamps over them.' (Abu Dawud 3230).

It was (and is) the culture of many places to go to the graves of saintly persons for superstitious motives, to beg the holy soul to help them become fertile, or make other requests. This is forbidden in Islam.

'May God curse the Jews who used the graves of their prophets as places of worship.' (Bukhari 23.60.414).

It is absolutely forbidden to ask the dead to answer one's prayers, or to seek to involve their aid, or to solicit their intercession. Stroking the grave with the hand, circumambulating it, and similar superstitious practices are also disapproved—these are acts which only lead to idolatry and giving 'partners' to God. The many venerated shrines to the relatives of the Blessed Prophet ﷺ and other faithful dead to be found in various places in the Islamic world are actually against the spirit of Islam.

The Blessed Prophet's ﷺ own grave was not originally inside the mosque at Madinah, but in the room of his wife Aishah, adjacent to it. Only later was the mosque building extended to include it—and many Islamic purists feel that this is wrong practice and should be rectified.

As regards the visitors to an ordinary family grave, the commendable prayer for a visitor is:

'Peace be upon you, O believers and Muslims who dwell here; we shall, God willing, be joining you. We ask God to grant well-being to us and to you.' (Muslim 2126).

It is also recommended to pray for forgiveness and

mercy for the dead.

Abu Hurayrah recorded that a negress (or young negro youth) who used to sweep the mosque died. The Prophet ﷺ missed him, and when he asked about him the people told him that he had died. He said: 'Why didn't you inform me?' Then he said: 'Lead me to his grave.' So they led him, and he prayed over him. (Abu Dawud 3197).

Abu Hurayrah recorded that the Apostle of Allah ﷺ visited his mother's grave and wept, and caused those around him to weep. The Apostle ﷺ then said: 'I asked my Lord's permission to pray for forgiveness for her, but I was not allowed. I then asked His permission to visit her grave, and I was allowed. So visit graves, for they make you mindful of death.' (Abu Dawud, 3228).

Aishah recorded a long and moving hadith about the Blessed Prophet ﷺ and his practice of visiting graveyards. He used to sometimes slip away in the middle of the night, and go to stand in prayer amongst his dead loved ones at the cemetery of Baqi.

Aishah said: 'When it was my turn for Allah's Messenger ﷺ to spend the night with me, he turned on his side, put on his mantle, took off his shoes and placed them near his feet, and spread the corner of his shawl on his bed, and then lay down till he thought I had gone to sleep. Then took hold of his mantle quietly and put on the shoes quietly, and opened the door and went out, and then closed it softly. I covered my head, put on my veil and tightened my waist wrapper, and then went out following his steps until he reached (the cemetery) Baqi.

He stood there, and he stood for a long time. He then lifted his hands three times, and then returned, and I also returned. He hastened his steps, and I also hastened my steps. He ran, and I too ran. He came (to the house) and I also came (to the house). I, however, got there before him and I entered and as I lay down on the bed he entered, and said: 'Why is it, O Aishah, that you are out of breath? I said: 'It is nothing.' He said: 'Tell me, or the Subtle and Aware will inform me!' I said: 'Messenger of Allah ﷺ, may my mother and father be ransom for you, and then I told him (the whole story). He said: 'Was it the darkness of your shadow that I saw in front of me?' I said: 'Yes.' He smacked me on the chest, causing me pain, and said: 'Did you think that Allah and His Apostle would deal unjustly with you?' (He meant by this to rebuke her for thinking that perhaps he was slipping away to see some other woman). She said: 'Even if humans conceal it, Allah will know it.' He said: 'Gabriel came to me when you saw me. He called me, and he concealed it from you. I responded to his call, but I also concealed it from you, as you were not fully dressed. I thought that you had gone to sleep and I did not like to awaken you, fearing that you might be frightened. Gabriel said: 'Your Lord has commanded you to go to the inhabitants of Baqi and pray forgiveness for them.' I said: 'Messenger of Allah (i.e. Gabriel), how should I pray for them?' He said: 'Say, Peace be upon the inhabitants of this city (graveyard) from among the believers and the Muslims, and may Allah have mercy on those who have gone ahead of us, and those who will come later on, and we shall, God willing, join you.' (Muslim 2127).

CONDOLENCES

Because Muslims should all have a strong faith in life after death, and the continued existence of their departed loved one, it is not considered appropriate to grieve too much. This would show a lack of obedience to the will of Allah, who took back that soul when it was His will. However, grief is inevitable for a loved one, and condolences may be offered to the bereaved for up to three days and nights after a death. The traditional formula is:

'May God make your reward abundant and your solace great, and grant forgiveness to the departed.'

To which the reply is:

'May God hear your prayer, and have mercy upon us and you.'

Muhammad ibn Sirin recorded that when one of the sons of Umm Atiyya died, and when it was the third day, she asked for yellow perfume and put it over her body, and said: 'We were forbidden to mourn for more than three days, except for our husbands.' (Bukhari 23.30.369).

Muslims are expected to mourn a husband (or wife) for four months and ten days (Bukhari 23.30.370).

We have reports of two cases of the Prophet's ﷺ

wives, Umm Habibah and Zaynab. The first lost her
father Abu Sufyan, and the other lost her brother. After
three days, they both requested perfume to wear. The
both said that they certainly did not ask for the
perfume because they wished to put on scent, but
simply because they had heard the Prophet ﷺ say: 'It
is not lawful for a woman who believes in Allah and
the Day of Judgement to be in mourning for any
deceased person for over three nights, except for her
husband, when the period is four months and ten
days.'

It is a kind practice if visitors to the bereaved
remember their sad state and do not make themselves
a burden by expecting food and meals to be prepared
for them. A kind visitor brings provisions with them.

Abdullah ibn Ja'far recorded the Apostle ﷺ as
saying: 'Prepare food for the family of Ja'far, for an
incident has come upon them and occupied them.'
(Abu Dawud 3126).

The common customs of holding gatherings during which the Qur'an is recited for three nights following the death, and of arranging a mourning celebration
and special gatherings or rawdahs on the day of the
death, or on the third day after it, or on the fortieth day,
or on the anniversary of the death, have no basis in the
Qur'an, the sunnah of the Blessed Prophet ﷺ or in the
practice of the early Muslims, may God have mercy on
them all.

VISITING THE GRAVES OF SAINTS

Visiting graves is only recommended to Muslims if it is for the purpose of expressing dutifulness to deceased parents and other loved ones, or to remind ourselves of the inevitability of death so that we can prepare for our lives to come. In that sense, the Prophet ﷺ referred to death and the grave as silent preachers.

Some people, however, take rather a superstitious attitude towards graves, particularly those of Muslims who are widely regarded as saints. They may particularly reverence the graves of those who had been relatives or companions of the Prophet ﷺ or famous holy people who lived at a particular place. It is important to realise that by raising these people to superhuman status, this constitutes in Islamic terminology a sort of worship.

While Muslims may not be aware that they are worshipping these human beings by their superstitions, the fact remains that by elevating them in this way they are in danger of taking themselves out of the fold of Islam. They are creating 'gods' from the ranks of human beings who were dedicated to the cause of Islam. Were those relatives and companions of the Prophet or great saints alive now, they would have certainly fought hard to convince these misled Muslims that their practice is not only wrong, but contradicts the very basis of the Islamic faith—the Oneness of Allah.

Moreover, it is not for us to classify dead people as saints or non-saints. Who are we to judge people, or to

know the real truth of their status? Some people may
have shown the appearance of being dedicated to
Allah, but how can we judge their intentions, their
secret hearts known only to Allah? A rich person may
dedicate a fortune to some charitable purpose, simply
in the hopes that people will admire him and respect
him. Someone who was less rich might only make a
small donation, and keep it secret, but it may have
represented a far greater sacrifice, and been done
solely for the purpose of pleasing Allah.

If people visit the tombs of persons they hope are
saints in the hope that they will have their wishes
fulfilled, what are they really thinking? They are
imagining that the dead person in the grave, or his
soul, has special privileges and powers, when in
reality they have no power; the visitor has appealed to
that person instead of appealing to Allah, Who alone
could help. In effect, he or she has committed shirk, by
trying to attribute a partner to Allah.

Some may think that although dead saints can do
nothing themselves, they could appeal to Allah on our
behalf. This is a nonsense; the dead are not intermedi-
aries between Allah and His servants. Such thoughts
are really polytheism, and forbidden to Muslim.

URS MUBARAK

Death-anniversary celebrations, particularly of
those thought to be saints, are popular in certain parts
of Islamic world, but are not at all recommended in
Islam. On the contrary, there is serious danger not only

of *shirk*, but also of deception and money-making. Should Muslims gather from all over the world to spend their money, indulge in unacceptable practices and thoughts, merely to have their wishes fulfilled by some dead person, on Allah's behalf? The idea is really preposterous.

'I am the least in need of a partner. If anyone associates a partner with Me, I abandon him to that partner.' (Hadith Qudsi).

If anyone has a dear wish, there is only one way of seeking Allah's help, namely to pray to Him directly.

> 'Your Lord says: 'Pray to Me, and I will answer you.' (40:60).

> 'When My servants ask you about Me, I am near; I respond to the supplication of anyone who prays to Me. Let them, therefore, respond to Me and believe in Me, so that they may be rightly guided.' (2:186).

Entreating any dead person to intercede on behalf of the living really takes that supplicant out of the fold of Islam.

RECITATIONS

The 'Fatihah' is a certain type of ritual in which people gather to read certain verses of the Qur'an and certain phrases of glorification of Allah thousands of times. This is often coupled with other rituals, such as the preparation of special food.

Such practices seem to be widespread in the Muslim world, but they have no basis whatsoever in Islam, and cannot be supported by any Quranic verse or hadith. As such, these practices are innovations, and although they are intended to show respect and piety, they are misguided. The Prophet 🕮 said: 'Beware of newly-invented matters. For every invention is an innovation, and every innovation is going astray.' (Abu Dawud and Tirmidhi). People who follow these practices are really in error, but they are rarely prepared to listen to advice on the subject, because there is such pressure from their communities to ignore those who object to these practices, and regard them as neglectful and disrespectful. The effect of the practices no doubt makes them feel they have discharged what their religion expects of them, but Islam does not have these rituals, and unless it is followed in the manner taught to us by the Prophet 🕮, it will not bear its proper fruit.

Had the Prophet 🕮 encouraged, or even permitted, the organizing of any type of function, or the assembly of relatives in particular places at particular times to offer their condolences, these practices would have been followed each time one of the Muslims of Madinah died. It would have been reported to us, particularly since a good number of the Prophet's 🕮 companions died while he was still living. People who teach otherwise are really responsible for the backwardness and burdensome-ness of so many Muslim communities.

Why should we commemorate the death of any person? Is it to renew our sorrow for their departure?

Or is it to organise some sort of occasion which we assume will generate some reward from Allah for our efforts, and that this reward will go to the deceased person?

If the deceased are dear to us, we will *always* remember them and can pray for them anywhere, on any day or any occasion, and ask Allah to forgive them, even during our obligatory prayers. Dutiful children may pray for their deceased parents every day of their lives.

The idea of hiring professional reciters of the Qur'an, bringing people to recite Qur'an near the grave or in the home of the bereaved, or even worse— taking turns to keep up Quranic recitation from the time of death until the following Friday in the belief that Allah will forgive the deceased on that day, are all gross abuses of Islam.

To imagine that people can prevent the angels from accomplishing the task Allah has assigned them to is a nonsense.

Moreover, to give financial reward for a person reciting the Qur'an is not permissible. It is forbidden to both the reciter and the one who employs him or her. The reciter should not receive wages for recitation, and the other person commits an offense by hiring him or her for that purpose. Therefore these traditions not only place an unnecessary burden on relatives, but they do not earn them any reward in return.

It is far better for the relatives of the deceased to pray Allah to forgive them as often as they wish,

without conforming to any social traditions associat-
ing such an action which the passage of so many days
(or even years).

ACTIONS ON BEHALF OF THE DEAD

Scholars are unanimous that those who are dead
can benefit by what living people may do in one or two
ways. Firstly, whatever the deceased persons initiated
during their lifetime may be completed on their behalf.

'What is credited to a believer of his actions and
good deeds after his death is any useful knowledge he
might have taught or spread, a God-fearing child he
might have left behind, a copy of the Qur'an he might
have left to an heir, a mosque he might have built, a
house he might have dedicated for use by travellers, a
stream he might have caused to run, a donation to
charity he might have set aside when he was enjoying
good health. All that catches up with him after his
death.' (Ibn Majah).

Secondly, others may pray for Allah to forgive
them, and perform charities or pilgrimages on their
behalf.

'Those who come after them, pray: 'Our Lord,
forgive us our sins, as well as those of our
brethren who preceded us in faith.' (59:10).

There are numerous hadiths which tell that a
number of companions of the Prophet ﷺ asked him
whether they could give sadaqah or fast or do the
pilgrimage on behalf of their dead relative, and he
always said that they could, and that the dead person

would benefit by it.

Sa'd ibn Ubadah, the chief of the Ansari tribe of al-Khazraj, said to the Prophet ﷺ: 'Messenger of Allah, my mother died when I was away. Would she benefit if I gave sadaqah on her behalf?' The Prophet ﷺ answered in the affirmative. Sa'd said: 'I would like you to be my witness that I am giving on her behalf my orchard at al-Meraf.' (Bukhari).

Abu Dawud, An-Nisai, Ahmad and others record the story of a woman who had pledged that if she was saved from drowning, she would fast for a month; she was saved, but died before she had done the promised fast. Her daughter, or sister, received permission from the Prophet ﷺ to carry out the fast on her behalf.

Hadiths in support of offering the pilgrimage on behalf of a deceased person or one who is unable to make the journey, are numerous.

If a person dies without settling a debt and leaves no money to settle it, anyone could pay it on his or her behalf. Whether the person paying it is a relative or not, the deceased is deemed to have repaid the debt.

> 'To Allah we belong, and to Allah we return.'
> (2:156; 28:70; 96:8).

Chapter 13

Eternal Life

Islam teaches that people who do not believe in the Day of Judgement and the Life to Come are making a very foolish assumption—they think that all the prophets and messengers sent by God to warn humanity of this ultimate destiny were mistaken. The Qur'an makes it very clear that one day, at a time when God sees fit and which is known only to Him, this world will indeed be brought to an end in a cosmic cataclysm that is beyond all imagination. On that Day, despite the scepticism of non-believers, the bodies of the dead will be reconstituted down to the least little detail:

> 'I call to witness the Day of Resurrection, and I call to witness the self-reproaching spirit, the conscience. Turn aside from evil! Do you humans think that I cannot re-assemble your bones? I promise you, I am able to put you together again in perfect order, even to the tips of your fingers.' (75:1-4)

This is a highly significant statement, since the science of the twentieth century has revealed that each person's fingers are completely unique, even in the cases of identical twins.

On the Day of Resurrection all humans who have

already died will be raised from their graves to be rejoined with their souls, while those who are still alive on earth will die and enter the same state. All will then stand before God to face judgement, each one as totally alone and helpless as when they came into the world.

> 'To God belongs the mystery of the heavens and the earth. The decision of the Hour of Judgement will be swift as the twinkling of an eye—for God has power over all things.' (16:77)

> 'Unbelievers say: 'This Hour will never come upon us!' Say: 'Nay! Most surely, but my Lord, it will come upon you; by Him who knows the Unseen, from Whom is not hidden the least little atom of the heavens or on earth.' (34:3).

The Prophet ﷺ told his listeners that the dead would be assembled barefooted, naked and uncircumcised. Aishah asked: 'Will the male and female be together on that Day, and will they be looking at each other?' Upon this, Allah's Messenger ﷺ said: 'Aishah, the matter would be too serious for them to look to one another!' (Muslim 6844).

This is a very interesting statement. Circumcision is something done to boys after their birth in human bodies. Every single male is, of course, born *uncircumcised* and it is in this original state, unaltered by hand of physician, that they are resurrected. It presumably also follows from this that people who have been literally carved up by the hazards of human life, who have lost limbs, or eyes, or kidneys, or skin surface, or whatever, *will find themselves restored* to the perfection of their creation. One might further assume that any human injured or damaged before birth, or in the process of birth, will also be restored. It is a very pleasant thought for those who have suffered physically and mentally from handicaps and horrifying wounds, burns, scarring, and so forth.

I have an interesting little anecdote which might be illustrative of this. A friend used to feed a blackbird that only had one leg. It became very tame, and learned certain little tricks, like pecking on the window. One day it disappeared, and she assumed it had fallen prey to a cat. However, the next day the pecking alerted her once more, and as she opened the window, the blackbird did not fly away but vanished before her eyes. And then, she realized that the bird had two legs.

Here's a moving report from a well-known cricketer who had a blind father. They were devoted to each other, and friends were shocked when the cricketer went out to play a match on the day of his father's funeral. It seemed so disrespectful. But the cricketer waved the disapproval aside. 'Don't you realise,' he said, 'that this will be first time my father *saw* me play?' The Prophet ﷺ said: 'Barefoot, naked and uncircumcised.' The mention of being naked, and male private parts, made Aishah react with modesty. Items of clothing are matters of this world, and are not granted an eternal existence! Naked we came into this world; and naked we enter the next. What our bodies will become, and with what they will be adorned, are matters of al-Ghayb.

In fact, Aishah was deeply affected by the thought of the Hereafter. Once, when she thought about Hell, she wept and the Apostle ﷺ asked her what was making her cry. 'She replied: 'I thought of Hell and wept. Will you remember your family on the Day of Resurrection?' He said: 'There are three places where no one will remember anyone—at the scale, until one knows whether his weight is light or heavy; at the (examination of) the Book when one is commanded (to) take and read Allah's record, until he knows whether his book will be put into his right hand, into his left hand or behind his back; and at the Path when it is placed across jahannam.' (Abu Dawud 4737).

At the Judgement, the Record that was compiled by the two angels who watched over him or her during lifetime is produced for each individual. This record took note of every detail of that person's life and thought.

> 'Angels are appointed over you to protect you; they are kind and honourable, and write down your deeds. They know and understand all that you do.' (82:10-12).

> 'Every person's judgement is fastened round his neck; on the Day We will bring forth a book which shall be shown wide open. Read your book; you have no need of anyone but yourself to work out your account.' (17:3-4).

Why should Allah have sanctioned the keeping of this record? Since Allah sees and knows everything, it is hardly for His benefit, to give Him the information on which to judge us! It is merely to prove matters to the individual souls, those who have forgotten their deeds, or think that they can escape judgement by a simple denial that they did those things, or who swear desperately that they never did them. They will be confronted by the record that shows every single thing documented in detail as it took place. Not the minutest thing, of deed, motivation, or consequence of the deed, is omitted.

Moreover, it is no use trying to foist the blame on others:

> 'Those whose lives the angels take in a state of wrongdoing to their own souls—then would they offer submission 'We did no evil!' Nay, truly, God knows all that you did.' (16:28).

> 'When Our messengers (of death) arrive and take their souls, they say: 'Where are those things that you used to invoke besides God?' They will reply: 'They have abandoned us.' And they will bear witness against themselves, that they had rejected God. He will say: 'Join the company of those who passed away before you—humans and jinns—into the Fire.' Every time a new People enters, it curses its sister-People (that went before) as they follow each other, all into the Fire. These last complain about the first: 'Our Lord! It is these that misled us! Give them a double penalty in the Fire!' He will say: 'Doubled for all!' Yet this you do not understand. Then those who went first will say to the newcom-

ers: 'See then! You have no advantage over us;
so taste the penalty for all that you did.' (7:37-
39).

For the souls of the righteous, including Aishah,
who wondered whether the resurrected Prophet ﷺ
would remember her, or know her, Allah revealed that
ultimately people who love each other will indeed be
reunited with their dear ones:

> 'On day He will gather them together; it will
> be as if they had waited for no more than an
> hour of a day; they will recognise each other.'
> (10:45)

Anas ibn Malik recorded that a desert Arab asked
Allah's Messenger ﷺ when the last hour would be?
Allah's Messenger ﷺ said: 'What preparations have
you made for it?' He said: 'The love of Allah and of His
Messenger.' Thereupon the Prophet ﷺ said: 'You will
be along with one whom you love.' (Muslim 6378; see
also 6379, 6380, 6382 and 6385).

People who have been happy together will find
their good relationships continuing, whereas people
who are not happy together will either be reconciled
and see each other differently, or may not be obliged to
be in their company.

'Abu Hurayrah recorded Allah's Messenger ﷺ as
saying: 'Souls are troops collected together, and those
who were at ease with each other would be drawn
close to one another, and those amongst them who
opposed each other would be separated from them.
(Muslim 6376).

However, on Judgement Day each person stands completely alone, powerless to plead for another, not even the closest and most loving and tolerant of relationships, a mother for a child, or a wife for a husband.

> 'One burdened soul shall not bear the burden of another. And even if the heavy-laden cry out for its burden to be carried, not one bit of it shall be carried, not even by the next of kin.' (35:18)

On what will they be judged? The Blessed Prophet ﷺ made it quite clear:

'On that Day, no step of a servant of God shall slip until they have answered concerning four things: their bodies and how they used them; their lives and how they spent them; their wealth and how they earned it; and their knowledge and what they did with it.'

Those who insisted on denying God and rejecting His guidance, who devoted themselves to the worship of other things, and spent their lives doing evil, will be consigned to a place which is completely alienated from God—and this will be a state of enduring torment and despair from which there will be no respite. They will long to have another chance to return to earth and try again, in the light of their new found knowledge of reality, but it will be too late.

> 'Truly, sinners will be in the punishment of Hell, to remain therein. It will not be lightened for them, and they will be overwhelmed with despair. We shall not be unjust to them, but it

is they who have been unjust to their own
souls.' (43:74-76)

On the other hand, a state of unutterable bliss and
serenity awaits those who left this life in a state of
surrender to Him.

'O My servants, no fear shall be on you that
day nor shall you grieve—those who have
believed in Our signs and submitted. Enter
the Garden, you and your wives, in rejoicing.'
(43:68-70).

Surah 37 gives a glimpse of the bewilderment and
confusion of those who have passed through death
into their new form of life, and the kind of discussions
they have:

'They will turn to one another and question
one another. One of them will start the talk
and say: 'I had a close friend (on earth) who
used to say—'What! Are you among those
who (believe in) the truth (of the Message)?
Why, when we die and become dust and
bones, (do you think,) we shall really receive
rewards and punishments?' A voice said:
'Would you like to look down (and see him)?'
He looked down, and saw (this friend) in the
midst of the fire. And he said (to that friend):
'By God! Truly you almost destroyed me
(too)—for had it not been for the grace of God
I should certainly have been among those
down there! But then (O my friends in Paradise) is it (really) so that we shall not die
(again), beyond our previous death, and that
we shall never (again) made to suffer?' Truly,
this—this indeed—is the triumph supreme!

To attain this, then, let them all strive, those
who labour (in God's way). (37:50-61).

However, there are merciful hints that even the
punishments of Hell do not necessarily last for ever:

'The hypocrites will be in the lowest depths of
the Fire; no helper will you find for them:
except for those who repent, mend, hold fast
to God, and purify their religion in God's
sight; if so, they will be with the believers, and
soon will God grant to the believers a reward
of immense value. What can God gain by your
punishment if you are grateful and you believe? No, it is God that recognises and knows
all things.' (4:145-147).

'The day it arrives, no soul shall speak except
by His leave; of those (gathered) some will be
wretched and some will be blessed. Those
who are wretched shall be in the Fire; there
will be for them therein the heaving of sighs
and sobs. They will remain therein for all the
time that the heavens and the earth endure,
except as thy Lord wills; for thy Lord is the
Accomplisher of what He plans.' (11:105-107).

Muslims believe that Heaven and Hell are not just
spiritual or psychic states, but in renewed bodies
which God will give us.

'It is He Who brings out the living from the
dead, and Who brings out the dead from the
living; and Who gives life to the earth after it
is dead; and thus shall you also be brought out
(from the dead).. And among His signs is this,
that when He calls you, by a single call, from
the earth—behold, you will straightaway come

forth..it is He Who begins creation, and then
repeats it; and for Him it is a simple matter.'
(30:19, 25, 27)

It is a completely different dimension, and we are
created afresh in a form beyond our knowledge. The
Muslim scholar al-Ghazzali recorded one beautiful
hadith in which the Prophet ﷺ inadvertently made an
old lady cry when he said: 'No old woman will enter
Paradise.' When the distressed lady wept, he added
gently: 'On that Day, you will not remain old. As Allah
said—I shall create them anew and make them young.'[1]

The Prophet ﷺ in fact stated on several occasions
that all righteous women, no matter how aged and
decayed they may have been on earth, will be resurrected as virginal maidens and will, like their male
counterparts, remain eternally young in Paradise.[2]

'We shall bring them into being in a life
renewed, having resurrected them as virgins,
full of love, well matched with those who
have attained righteousness.' (56:35-37)

The inevitable change of physical form and being
is stated clearly in 56:60-61:

'We have created death to be in the midst of
you, and We will not be prevented from
changing your forms and creating you again
in forms you know not.' (56:60-61)

---

1. Al-Ghazzali, 'Book of Destructive Evils,' p. 123.

2. These traditions are quoted in full of Tabari and Ibn Kathir and well
illustrate 56:36; in the next verse the words 'well-matched' indicate
equal age—the meaning adopted by most commentators—as (see also
38:52 and 78:33) well as of equal quality.

Abu Sa'id al-Khudri and Abu Hurayrah recorded Allah's Messenger ﷺ as saying: 'There will be an announcer (in Paradise) who will make this announcement: Truly! There is in store for you (everlasting) health, and that you should never fall ill, and that you live (for ever) and do not die at all. And that you would remain young and never grow old...'. (Muslim 6803)

This lovely picture of the future life is always before the mind and consciousness of the devout Muslim. The awareness keeps the whole of earthly life, whether intensely happy or in deepest pain, in perspective. Earthly life is passing, temporary , and only a test for the future.

The value of this world in comparison to the Hereafter is no more than that of a single droplet in the ocean. The Blessed Messenger ﷺ once said:

'By Allah! This world (is so insignificant in comparison) to the Hereafter that (it is as) if one of you should dip his finger in the ocean and then he should see what has stuck to it.' (Muslim 6843).

Once the Prophet ﷺ was walking through the bazaar when he came across a dead lamb with very short ears. He took hold of its ear and said:

'Who amongst you would like to buy this lamb for one dirham?' They said: 'We would not like to have it for even less than that, as it is of no use to us.' He said: Wouldn't you have it (if it was free of any cost)?' They said: 'By Allah, not even if it were alive, for there is defect in it, its ear is very short; and it is dead also.'

Thereupon Allah's Messenger ﷺ said: 'By Allah! This world is more insignificant in the eye of Allah as this dead lamb is in your eye.' (Muslim 7059).

The reality of one's true state in the Hereafter renders all the passing joys or sorrows of earth down to their right perspective. Our transitory suffering and pains even terrible traumatic sufferings and heart-aches, will be forgotten in the light of God's Presence:

'That person..who had led the most miserable life (in the world) on joining the people of Paradise and being made to dip once in Paradise, if it was said to him: 'O son of Adam, did you face any hardship? Or did any distress fall to your lot?' he would say: 'By Allah, no, O my Lord, never did I face any hardship or experience any distress.' (Muslim 6738, on the authority of Anas ibn Malik). The memory of all that pain has gone.

The Qur'an gives detailed descriptions of what it will be like in Heaven in terms that are familiar to us, terms of this life and its luxuries, but we must remember that the luxuries and happiness of Heaven are actually much more than we can visualise. Had Allah described them as they actually are, we would not have understood His description, our life-experience is too modest to comprehend it.

Some people with a peculiar attitude towards women (and please remember that over 50% of the Muslim community are women) have wondered whether women will have the same rewards in Heaven

as men; whether there will be sexual relationships;
what exactly are Huris, and how women in Heaven
will react to seeing their husbands greeted by Huris
(beautiful female spirit beings). Some writings have
suggested that male Muslims in Heaven will have
enormous sexual prowess, and will spend their time in
using up one fresh virgin after another—one wonders
if this would really be a suitable after-death occupation
for a man who had spent his earthly life trying to
control his passions and retain his sexuality within
marriage! And what will happen to all the poor virgins
once they have been used?

That the Qur'an uses the masculine reference
when it speaks of Allah's reward to believers is no
more than a requirement of the Arabic language—as it
is in many other languages. Allah makes it abundantly
clear that the same rewards will be given to male and
female Muslims for the same actions. One should read
all references to reward in the Hereafter that occur in
the masculine gender as equally applicable in the
feminine gender:

> 'As for anyone, man or woman, who does
> righteous deeds and is a believer, him We
> shall most certainly cause to live a good life;
> and most certainly We shall grant to such as
> these their reward in accordance with the best
> they ever did.' (16:97).

> 'For all men and woman who have
> surrendered themselves to Allah, and all
> believing men and women, and all truly
> devout men and women, and all men and

women who are true to their word, and all
men and women who are patient in adversity,
and all men and women who humble
themselves before Allah, and all men and
women who give in charity, and all men and
women who fast, and all men and women
who are mindful of their chastity, and all men
and women who remember Allah unceasingly;
for all of them Allah has truly made ready
forgiveness of sins and a great reward.' (33:35).

When the Qur'an speaks of wives for believers in
Heaven, incidentally, this may or may not refer to the
marriages of this world. Certainly, if a married couple
are good believers and they are both admitted to
Heaven, they may be together in Heaven if they
wish it.

'As for those who have attained to
righteousness..(they will find themselves)
amidst fruit-laden lote-trees and flower-clad
acacias, extended shade and gushing waters,
abundant fruit never failing and never out of
reach. And (with them will be their) spouses,
raised high; for behold, We shall have brought
them into being in a renewed life, having
resurrected them as virgins, full of love, well-
matched with those who have attained righteousness; a good may of olden times, and a
good may of later times. (56:27-40).

Verse 34 is the key verse mentioning spouses.
Some commentators use the literal translation couches
here, and render it 'on raised couches' instead of
'spouses raised high.' However, many of the most
outstanding commentators (e.g. Baghawi, Zamakshani,

Razi, Baydawi, etc.) support the meaning 'spouses.' They do this for two main reasons—the connecting statement in the next verse (i.e. couches are not created afresh as virgins!), and because 'firash' (lit. bed or couch) in the classical Arabic idiom is frequently used to denote 'wife' or 'husband.' Zamakshani draws particular attention to 36:56 which refers to the inmates of Paradise reclining on couches in happiness, 'they and their spouses.'

What about the Huris mentioned in 56:22 and elsewhere? (38:52; 44:54; 52:20; 55:72) What are they, and how are female believers supposed to react to them? Will they not jeopardise a wife's happiness? One can read fantasies and theories churned out by presumably sex-starved pious gentlemen who genuinely believe they are in for a really amazing sexual 'good time' with these girls in Heaven.

Sadly for hem, they have got it wrong. The 'Hur' of 56:22 is most likely to be identified with the 'spouse raised high' of 56:34. The noun 'hur' (pure companion) is the plural of both ahwar (male) and hawra' (female), either of which terms describes 'a person distinguished by hawar—which primarily devotes intense whiteness of the eyeball and lustrous black of the iris of the eye. In a general sense hawar signifies simply 'whiteness,' or in the moral sense, 'purity' (cf. Tabari, Razi and Ibn Kathir in their explanation of hawariyyun in 3:52.) 'Huri' means 'pure beings most beautiful of eyes.' Razi commented that the use of the word 'eye' here may actually refer to 'soul,' since the eye in a sense 'reflects' the state of the soul. So, it may be that 'hur 'in' means 'companion pure of soul' and not necessarily a female at all.

However, most commentators regard it as a feminine thing; many of the earliest understood it to signify the righteous human women raised to Paradise and not a different order of beings to be found in Paradise.

So, what about sex? Sadly for those who hoped otherwise, sex is only part of the realm of the physical. In the earthly life Allah made sex enjoyable in order to ensure the survival of the species. This is no longer relevant in life in the Hereafter. People in Heaven will not go on giving birth to children and increasing their own numbers. At no time does the description of Heaven given in the Qur'an mention children being born to believers.

Well, supposing we can now accept that if we choose, we may continue to associate with the person who was our earthly spouse when we are in Paradise. What will be the case for those who have had more than one beloved wife or husband? People are frequently very possessive about their spouses, and dislike the thought that a partner could love somebody else as well as themselves. Young people, in particular, with their sentimental and emotional attitude towards romantic love, find this hard to contemplate. However, as we grow older, we all know it is perfectly possible to love any number of children equally, and as we pass through our earthly lives, it is quite possible to love someone and then lose them, and then love again without in any way turning against our love for the first person. No doubt in Heaven, without the jealousies often attached to sexual relationships, people who have loved more than once, or married more than once, will be bound by a feeling of close relationship to all of them.

We cannot begin to imagine our future state of existence, any more than a person holding a seed in his hand could possibly imagine what sort of plant or tree it would grow into—huge oak tree, delicate orchid, humble blade of grass? Or how could an adult frog convey to an infant tadpole what life was like outside the environment of the pond? The tadpole has no experience of it, and cannot possibly imagine what it must be. The tadpole may not even be aware that it is going to become a frog.

Similarly, the butterfly cannot convey information about its butterfly-life to the caterpillar, crawling around a leaf. One day every caterpillar wraps itself in a shroud of its own making, and becomes a crysallis or cocoon. There is the cocoon, a silent, still and apparently lifeless thing. Yet there comes a moment when it is split and cast aside, and out of it emerges the most beautiful creature, the butterfly.

So it is with our bodies. They are just like tiny seeds, which will be placed into the earth and out of them will come forth whatever beautiful and wonderful from Allah has already programmed within them— and the dry husk, no longer needed to contain them, will simply be cast aside.

'It is God who is in the splitting of the seed-
grain and the sprouting of the date-stone,
Who causes the living to come from the dead...
Who splits the daybreak from darkness.' (6:95-
96).

The seemingly dead body is no more than a cocoon, ready to be shed and cast aside by the spirit within—so, when we look at a body, we are not really seeing our loved one, but only their 'empty shell.' And although we may miss that 'shell' for a while, what reason is there to grieve?

The mortal remains of our loved ones will go back to being the earth of which they came, until such time as God sees fit to call them out again and reform them and we have His promise that He can restore anyone He wishes in full detail, even to their finger-prints. Meanwhile, the souls of our loved ones will fly away to experiences we cannot know. These are happy thoughts, full of consolation, hope and joy.

Finally, brothers and sisters, let us remember that our times are unknown to us; they may be short or long—we have no way of predicting. It is no use expecting to be able to put off to tomorrow what we ought to be doing today. That tomorrow might never come. If we are Muslim, we know that whenever we say of a thing 'I will do it later,' we must add 'insha' Allah'—if God wills (18:23-24).

People who have had personal contact with death find that it changes their awareness of life. Conscious awareness brings with it a new appreciation of life. I have a personal similitude of a beautiful set of cups

and saucers. They were given to me when I got
married, and I put them aside 'for best,' saving them
up for some future occasion. After twenty-three years
of marriage my life changed and my husband and I
were divorced. Unpacking my cupboards and discovering this marriage-gift which had never been used
was one very sad detail of this experience which
taught me a lesson. My time of marriage had come and
gone, and the gift was still unwrapped!

Life *before* death is important. Let us try hard to live
every day as it comes, accepting each new dawn as a
fresh gift from our dear Lord, full of opportunities and
chances to do good and kind things to those we love.
Let us not waste our time, or find ourselves called back
to God with any of His gifts 'unwrapped'!

If we are angry or disappointed with someone,
help us to love them more and try to change the
situation. If we are impatient with someone, give us
the grace to remember that God is pleased with snails
and tortoises just as much as with race-horses and
greyhounds. If we are short-tempered with someone,
help us to find patience and sympathy, for one of the
hardest things bereaved people have to face is their
guilt—the many 'if only's,' the many times they have
said things that should not have been said, or not said
the things that should have been said; done things that
should not have been done, and not done the things
which should have been done.

Help us to live every day *as if it was our last*. Help
us to accept each new day as a gift, and not to waste it.

Help us always to use our time to love, and to bring peace, and to heal, and to reconcile, and to work hard for the bringing of Your will on earth. Help us to love and appreciate those whom You have given to us, and to cherish them while we have time.

Help us to accept them, knowing that we might not have chosen ourselves the particular character given to our brother or sister, or parent or child, but that this choice was not ours to make, but Yours. If a relative distresses or disappoints us, help us to love them *more*, and not cast them aside and then regret it later.

Help us always to remember You, that we may dedicate our lives to Your full service—not out of any fear, but out of love for the One Who is Most Perfect, the Lord of the Unseen, the Lord of this life and the life to come. Amen.

Chapter 14

Poems of Grief and Consolation

FAREWELLS

Your guest is going soon. Who has the knowledge
of that day you and I shall meet again? Only the
   One.
All things are but the flowing of a river,
the joys of our sweet yesterdays are dreams;
although we try, we cannot keep them tight,
cannot hold them captive in the hand,
even though the pains of our todays rack us with
   sorrow.
You cannot cut the water with a knife;
without a moment's ceasing, it flows on.

In the fresh light, to the peeping of tiny chickens,
we take our breakfast on the charpoys,
aware of endings and beginnings.
While we sit together it is summer still, and we can
   think
'If only life were always like this!' Ah, the pain
of these 'if only' thoughts. We sit there, silent.
Words are only so much clutter—skimming insects
on a pool—never expressing what they truly mean.

When I have gone, memories will come with
   dawns,

flooding back on fragile wings of light.
You ask when I will come again? I do not know.
Shall we ever sit again, in this our meaningful
            silence?
There is a long road winds before each traveller,
seeming its longest on the morn of parting.

My heart in misery is upside down.
Goodbye, my friend. What, after all, is parting?
Nothing but the waving of a hand,
a focus of the eye to a new distance.

Wherever my feet take me, you will come,
I'll hear your music, the lilt of it so melancholy
that long before it ends my tears will spring
like mountain streams, like mercury in sunlight.
If I could grasp the sunlight, I would give
it happily to you. O fare thee well;
Oh, if only, if only it could never end.
Even before I've gone, I mourn your loss, my friend.

LISTEN TO THE REED

'Listen to the reed forlorn crying
ever since it was torn
from its rushy bed a strain
of eternal love and pain.
If you would know how lovers bleed,
listen, listen to the reed.'
Mevlana Jalal ud-Din Rumi, Qonya.

The reed-bed sighs; and in my heart a shifting
like the wind moving the green fingers of the
            rushes.
Water purls and ripples, splashes over stones.

It is a peaceful sound, but in my heart
there is no peace. For there's a wound
as sharp and jagged as the knife that cuts
the reed, tears out its life, so it becomes
no more a living thing, but just a hollow tube.

There is no place for fear, only for sorrow—
sorrow for the blindness of the world
that weighs so heavy, like the blindness of a stone;
sorrow for the passing of the day
that did not bear fruit, and will become a husk;
sorrow for the thorn piercing my heart
that did not mean to pierce me, but my blindness
drove me on, and made me fall on it.

Listen to the reed; there is a sighing
over all the world, if we have ears to hear.
Where is the heart that has not known the thorn,
the pod that has not spilled the myriads of seed
then withered up and dried? Where is the stone
that has not lain a thousand years till smashed
by iron hammers? Listen to the reed—

There is a sound that pierces even iron,
a sad, immortal cry of grief that's known
instinctively in every cell split from its fellow;
life is like the rain sent from the sky
snatched greedily by every rush and leaf;
you see them swell and bloom and then
become dry stubble, scattered by the wind.

O brave show, life, to flourish for a season
then be gone; even the stone is fleeting
upon this wide sphere turning, wheeling round,
dancing to the music of the Eternal Reed.

There is no striving but to hear the tune
and dance, gripped in the tight melancholy of flesh
that wraps us like a shroud. One day we'll see
mountains laid low, vibrating earth shorn down—
bereft of landmark, bare of all the reeds—
and naked, as the hour of first creation, we shall
        stand
and know the music, slip into the dance, the stream.

Ah love, the separation is a bitter thing—
soul torn from soul, and every soul from Thee.
To live, and to be separate, is pain—and the earth cries,
a split-off reed that now, an instrument, gives voice.
O soul, if you would know how lovers bleed
then listen, listen, listen to the reed.

AMR ALLAH—AT YOUR COMMAND, O LORD

She sits in the window, swathed in a cashmere
        shawl—
hungry for warmth—for she is frail, and very old,
maybe a hundred years. Her mist-filled eyes
gaze out across the valley to the resting-place
of all her dead, the white flecks of the gravestones
of seven children, nine of her grandchildren,
and at the last, her man. All buried, one by one.

Outside, the bulbuls and hoopoes come to feast
on apricots, and flutter to the birdbath,
preening and singing, scattering the water in spray.
By the garden's edge, in gathering dusk
small white butterflies are being blown about
like tiny scraps of paper, so much litter—
        yet the pairs
will not be sundered; as if joined by string
they always reunite again and flutter, two by two.

Such fragile trembling things, and yet life's fires
catch the last rays and burn brightly in their wings,
fires that died within her years ago, and left
this heap of burnt-out ash, this pain.

The day is gone, the light is gone, all
the warmth of my life is gone. My Lord, see—
        I'm alone.
So sad, to be alone and have to walk
this long, sad distance down this desolate hillside,
to those long-loved oases where for all those years
our dream-caravans pulled up and paused to drink,
idylls for which we never lost—in all those years—
our wild nostalgic yearning.

Where are the rooks? See, now they've left the sky,
and in a little while I'll see the first pinprick of
            lamps
piercing the dark like stars, then three then four.
Like distant campfires. Lord, let me sit still,
and play at death—not moving, like a lizard.
See, I have practised this so many times.

A lapwing starts up in the mustard fields.
Be off to bed, you foolish bird, while I remember
            now
the bustle in the women's tents, the young brides
            peering
into the swaying skins to see the yoghurt; all my
            daughters
squatting beside the open fires, stirring the pot; and
            me,
turning on the spit a freshly butchered lamb.

See, all the babies in my life blurring together in one
            muddle

of happy clamorous faces, sleeping in one pile.
Lord, I'm tired now, how can I count those faces,
or separate my own from all the others?

And where's my man? Where's he—my shining
          blade—
who gave into my maiden hands the gift
of his bright youth and then his middle years,
and by the hearth the comfort of his age? O, surely
          soon,
at God's command, we'll lie together, soon, and
          turn to dust—
once more together in each other's arms.

See! Who's that standing just beyond the door?
You? O handsome man, my love, can it be really
          you?
So many years I've waited, now I see your face!
After all these years you have come back for me?
A hundred years I've been here on this earth. I
          thought
by now the Lord had quite forgotten me. O Allah,
          here I am!
Your Ruqaiyyah is here, and so alone. At Your
          command,
I'm ready, Lord. You could have come for me
so many years ago.

See, now my strength has ebbed away, I am no
          more
than a snail's shell, yet here am I—oh see!
I am expectant, like a bride about to know my man
and run into his arms for the first time. Look, see my
          feet
are eager for the journey. All my life I've waited;

raise up Your arm, O Allah, give me leave! See, here
        I come—
running the first steps on my longed-for journey
        home.

IF I SHOULD DIE

Rabbana, if I should die one morning,
and find I had not died, but left my weak
and pain-wracked mortal frame wrapped snug and
        neat
upon the bed in the tight sheet of night,
while my true self, my body made of light—
with glowing joy and disbelief at that
which must be more than tongue could ever
        speak—
came drifting to the Place where angels sing,

and other female souls, wide-eyed and shy,
come—scarcely recognising—to the kiss
of willow-slim young warriors that they won
the hearts of long ago, with all the years
that brought them to the anguished parting tears
of cherished age now just a morning mist
dispersing with the rising of the sun,—
O then, like a lost child, I'd stand and cry—

I would look straightaway for him that You
gave me on earth. Maybe, on Your high throne,
You'd glance down at this clamouring and noise
spoiling Your peace, and notice from above
in all this vast throng—me! O dear my Lord,
and Watcher all my life, see—I'm alone!
I trust, my King, who knows me through and
        through,

You'll not delay but grant Your blessed word,
sent me the angels with their blazing eyes
to point me through this crowd towards my love.

Instead of which, maybe, after the thump
cascading down the black tunnel of night,
I'd wake and find I had no need to beg
a-searching through that magic wondrous land,
but, after all,—stretch out my fearful hand—
and, moulded to my back, there is the lump
of flesh I love, and there's the longed-for sight,
a face, all stubble now, and jagged prickle,
a corn-field in the month after the sickle—
and yokes of iron clamp around my leg.

I'm aching like the earth, I cannot wait.
Rouse up this lazy farmer, tell him 'Now!
Put down your narghileh, shake out your dreams,
and hurry, hurry, hurry to the plough.'

O Allah,
grant forgiveness to (this our dead loved one);
let him arise to the company of those who have followed Your
path in righteouness;
let him become a guide and a helper to those he has left
behind.
Forgive us, and him, O Lord of the Universe;
make his grave spacious, and grant him light in it.

Hadith Muslim 2003

Goodword Books

Tell Me About the Prophet Muhammad (HB)

Tell Me About the Prophet Muhammad (PB)

Tell Me About the Prophet Musa (HB)

Tell Me About Hajj (HB)

Tell Me About Hajj (PB)

Honeybees that Build Perfect Combs

The World of Our Little Friends, the Ants

Life Begins (PB)

The First Man (HB)

The First Man (PB)

The Two Brothers (HB)

The Two Brothers (PB)

The Ark of Nuh (HB)

The Ark of Nuh (PB)

The Brave Boy (PB)

Allah's Best Friend (PB)

The Travels of the Prophet Ibrahim

The Origin of Life (Colouring Book)

The First Man on the Earth (Colouring Book)

The Two Sons of Adam (Colouring Book)

The Ark of Nuh and the Animals (Colouring Book)

The Brave Boy (Colouring Book)

Allah's Best Friend (Colouring Book)

The Travels of the Prophet Ibrahim (Colouring Book)

The Ark of Nuh and the Great Flood (Sticker Book)

The Story of the Prophet Nuh (HB)

The Story of the Prophet Nuh (PB)

The Blessings of Ramadan (PB)

The Story of Prophet Yusuf

Stories from the Quran

The Holy Mosques

The Holy Quran (PB)

The Holy Quran (Laminated Board)

The Holy Quran (HB)

A Dictionary of Muslim Names

The Most Beautiful Names of Allah (HB)

The Most Beautiful Names of Allah (PB)

The Pilgrimage to Makkah

One Religion

Islamic Economics

The Story of Islamic Spain (PB)

The Travels of Ibn Battuta

Humayun Nama

Islamic Sciences

Islamic Thought...

The Qur'an for Astronomy

Arabic-English Dictionary for Advanced Learners

The Spread of Islam in the World

A Handbook of Muslim Belief

The Muslims in Spain

The Moriscos of Spain

Spanish Islam (A History of the Muslims in Spain)

A Simple Guide to Muslim Prayer

A Simple Guide to Islam

A Simple Guide to Islam's Contribution to Science

The Quran, Bible and Science

Islamic Medicine

Islam and the Divine Comedy

The Travels of Ibn Jubayr

The Arabs in History

Decisive Moments in the History of Islam

My Discovery of Islam

Islam At the Crossroads

The Spread of Islam in France

The Islamic Art and Architecture

The Islamic Art of Persia

The Hadith for Beginners

How Greek Science Passed to Arabs

Islamic Thought and its Place in History

Muhammad: The Hero As Prophet

A History of Arabian Music

A History of Arabic Literature

The Quran

Selections from the Noble Reading

The Koran

Allah is Known Through Reason

The Miracle in the Ant

The Miracle in the Immune System

The Miracle of Creation in Plants

The Miracle in the Spider

Eternity Has Already Begun

Timelessness and the Reality of Fate

Ever Thought About the Truth?

Crude Understanding of Disbelief

Quick Grasp of Faith

Death Resurrection Hell

The Basic Concepts in the Quran

The Moral Values of the Quran

Heart of the Koran

Muhammad: A Mercy to All the Nations

The Sayings of Muhammad

The Beautiful Commands of Allah

The Beautiful Promises of Allah

The Muslim Prayer Encyclopaedia

After Death, Life!

Living Islam: Treading the Path of Ideal

A Basic Dictionary of Islam

The Muslim Marriage Guide

GCSE Islam—The Do-It-Yourself Guide

The Soul of the Quran

Presenting the Quran

The Wonderful Universe of Allah

The Life of the Prophet Muhammad

History of the Prophet Muhammad

A-Z Steps to Leadership

The Essential Arabic

A Case of Discovery

Printed in India